CHANGING WORLD WORKBOOK

Leaving Certificate CORE Geography

CHARLES HAYES

Gill & Macmillan

Gill & Macmillan Ltd
Hume Avenue
Park West
Dublin 12
with associated companies throughout the world
www.gillmacmillan.ie

© Charles Hayes 2012
978 07171 5323 7

Design and print origination in Ireland by Design Image

For permission to reproduce photographs, the author and publisher gratefully
acknowledge the following:

© Alamy: 12, 22, 26, 27TR, 38, 39CL, 39CR, 39BR, 56TL, 56TR, 67TC, 67TR, 103C,
161TL, 161BR, 177; © Corbis: 32, 149, 161CB; © Finbarr O'Connell: 80B, 85;
© Getty Images: 39BL, 67BR, 103T, 103B, 119, 161TR, 161CT, 161BL; © Ordnance
Survey Ireland: 79B, 80T; © Peter Barrow: 83; © Science Photo Library: 27TL, 27TC,
67CR; Courtesy of NASA: 101; Courtesy of the State Examinations Commission: 46, 63.

The author and publisher have made every effort to trace all copyright holders, but if any
has been inadvertently overlooked we would be pleased to make the necessary
arrangement at the first opportunity.

Contents

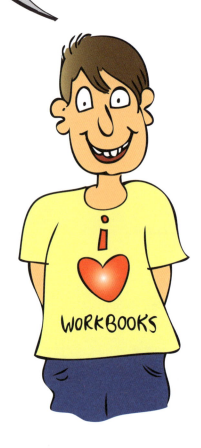

1 | Plate Tectonics

1 Structure of the earth

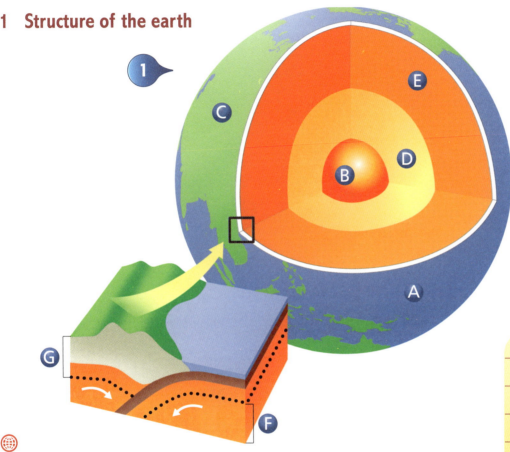

Inner core	
Mantle	
Oceanic crust	
Continental crust	
Outer core	
Lithosphere	
Asthenosphere	

(a) Examine the diagram of the structure of the earth in Figure 1. Match each of the terms in the grid with the correct letter in the diagram.

(b) Outline two differences between continental crust and oceanic crust.

(i) _____

_____

_____

(ii) _____

_____

_____

2   Plate tectonics

Examine the map of global plates in Figure 2 and answer the questions that follow.

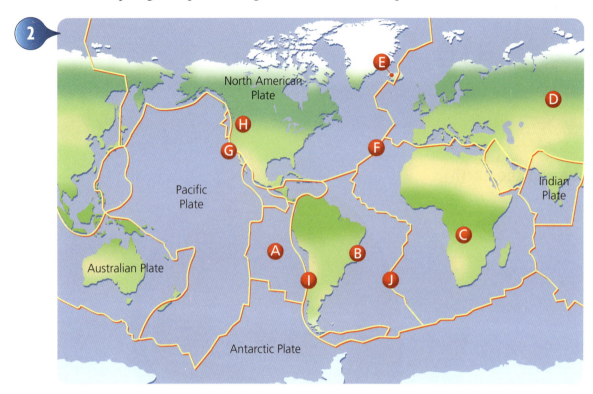

(a) Name the plates labelled **A**, **B**, **C** and **D** on the map.

A _____   B _____

C _____   D _____

(b) Name the island labelled **E** where volcanoes occur. _____

(c) Name the feature that can be found at **F**. _____

(d) Which of the labels **G**, **H**, **I** and **J** point to each of the following features?

● A constructive margin   _____

● A destructive margin   _____

● A transverse margin   _____

● A ridge of fold mountains   _____

3 Sea floor spreading

Examine the diagram shown in Figure 3. Then answer the questions that follow.

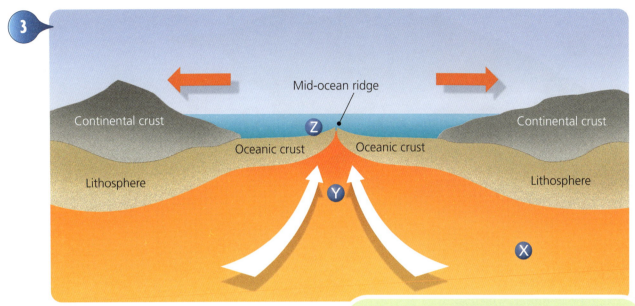

Alternative terms

- **Endogenic** is another word for *internal* processes. They include folding and volcanism and happen beneath the earth's surface.
- **Exogenic** is another word for *external* processes. They include weathering and erosion, and happen on or above the earth's surface.

(a) Name the earth's internal layer labelled **X**. _____

(b) Name the **internal** process shown by the arrows at **Y**. _____

(c) Name one mid-ocean ridge that you have studied. _____

(d) Name the type of plate boundary shown at **Z**. _____

(e) Two theories combine to make up the theory of *continental drift*.
One of these theories is that of *sea floor spreading*. Name and briefly describe the other theory. (Your description should contain no more than four sentences.)

- Name of theory: _____

- Description: _____

_____

_____

_____

_____

_____

4   A destructive plate boundary

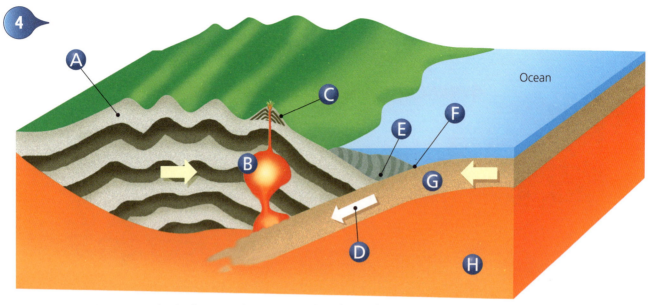

Examine Figure 4, which shows a destructive plate boundary.

(a) Match each of the terms in the box with the correct letter in the diagram.

Terrane	
Fold mountains	
Subduction	
Ocean trench	

Batholith	
Volcanic mountain	
Earth's mantle	
Oceanic crust	

(b) In the grid provided below, list three processes and three landforms
associated with destructive plate boundaries. Also list two places where
destructive plate boundaries can be found.

	Processes		Landforms		Places
1		1		1	
2		2		2	
3		3			

(c) Explain briefly why the plate boundary shown in Figure 4 is referred to as
'destructive'.

_____

_____

_____

5   Use the diagram in Figure 5 to explain the theory of plate tectonics.

_____

_____

_____

_____

_____

_____

_____

_____

_____

_____

_____

_____

_____

_____

_____

_____

5

6   (a)   Name the type of plate boundary that is illustrated
        in Figure 6.

        _____

        (b)   Name two geological processes or events that are likely
        to occur at such a plate boundary.

        •   _____

        •   _____

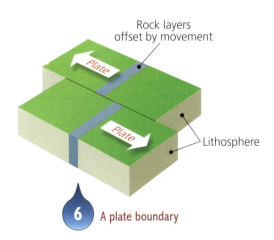

Rock layers offset by movement

Plate

Plate

Lithosphere

6   A plate boundary

Exam training
Answering a thirty-mark Higher Level question

Many Higher Level Leaving Certificate questions are *multi-part questions*. These questions are divided into three parts, two of which carry 30 marks each. The question below is a 30-mark question that appeared in a Leaving Certificate exam.

● Study the **question**.

● Study the official **marking scheme** for the question, which is shown below.

● Then examine the **sample answer**, which was allocated full marks in the examination.

● Later, use the experience you gain to help you write 30-mark answers of your own.

The question

 '*Plate boundaries are zones where crust is both created and destroyed.*'
Examine the above statement, with reference to examples you have studied. (30 marks)

The official marking scheme

This question requires that you examine plate boundaries where crust is being *created* **and** plate boundaries where crust is being *destroyed*.

The marking scheme is as follows:

● **Name one example** of a plate boundary where crust is created = **2 marks**

● **Name one example** of a plate boundary where crust is destroyed = **2 marks**

● **Thirteen SRPs*** are required in your examination of the given statement. At least six of these SRPs should refer to the situation where crust is being created and at least six SRPs should refer to the situation where crust is destroyed. Each SRP is given 2 marks = **26 marks**.

> * SRP stands for **Significant Relevant Point**. Each SRP should provide *a clear piece of geographical information that is to the point of the question asked.*

This question does not require diagrams, but a maximum of 6 marks (the equivalent of 3 SRPs) could be allowed for relevant and well-labelled diagrams.

Important!

When answering questions such as this, try where possible to **exceed the number of SRPs** normally required. Some of your SRPs may not be awarded marks, so it is useful to have two or three extra ones.

A full-mark sample answer

A destructive plate boundary (where crust is destroyed) can be found on the west margin of South America. — *Example: 2 marks*

At this boundary, convection currents of magma in the earth's mantle cause the west-moving South American Plate to collide with the east-moving Nazca Plate. ✔ The Nazca Plate is made up of oceanic crust, while the South American Plate is made up of continental crust at the boundary in question. ✔ Because oceanic crust is heavier than continental crust, the Nazca Plate sinks beneath the South American Plate at the point of collision. ✔ This sinking process is called subduction. ✔ When the oceanic plate sinks into the hot mantle it begins to melt and so is destroyed. ✔ Some of the molten plate material then forms huge underground bubbles of magma called batholiths. ✔ Molten magma from the batholiths sometimes forces its way to the surface to eventually form volcanic mountains. ✔

A constructive plate boundary (where crust is created) can be found beneath the middle of the Atlantic Ocean. — *Example: 2 marks*

At this boundary, convection currents of magma in the earth's mantle cause the North and South American Plates to move away from the Eurasian and African Plates. ✔ This parting movement is called divergence and goes on at about the same rate that our fingernails grow. ✔ As the plates separate, molten magma from the mantle emerges steadily through the cracks and fissures formed. ✔ This magma cools quickly on contact with the Atlantic seawater and creates new crust. ✔ This new crust becomes gradually wider as the plates continue to move apart. ✔ It is at its newest in the centre of the Mid-Atlantic Ridge and becomes gradually older towards the eastern and western edges of the Atlantic. ✔

> This full-mark answer did not include (or need) diagrams. The diagram below *could* have been adapted to score a maximum equivalent to three SRPs.

Examples: 2 @ 2 marks = 4 marks
SRPs (7 + 6) = 13 @ 2 marks = 26 marks
Total marks = 30/30

 7

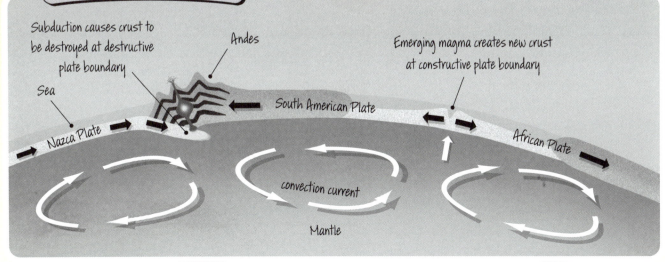

1

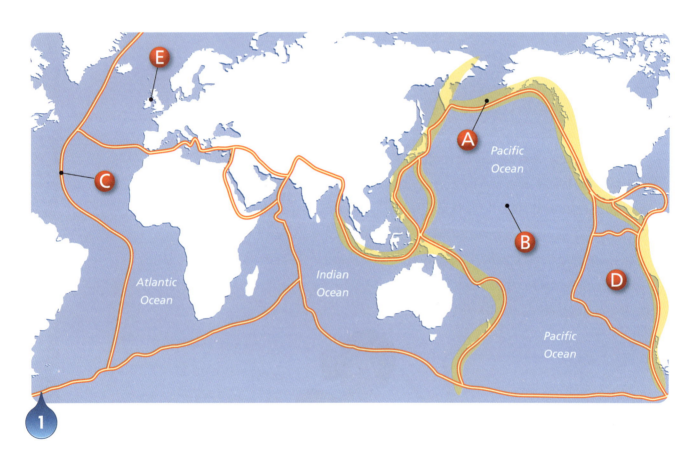

1

Examine the map in Figure 1.

(a) Match each of the labels **A–C** with the correct description.

(i) A place where plates are separating and where a volcanic mid-ocean   _____
ridge has formed.

(ii) The Pacific Ring of Fire – one of the most volcanically active parts   _____
of the world.

(iii) A place where volcanic islands are situated over an isolated hot spot.   _____

(b) Name the crustal plate labelled **D**. _____

(c) Name the plateau labelled **E**. _____

2 Explain how the study of plate tectonics has helped us to understand the global distribution of volcanoes.

Marking scheme

- Two global examples identified @ 2 marks each = 4 marks
  13 SRPs* @ 2 marks each = 26 marks
  Total = **30 marks**

(The equivalent of 2 SRPs (4 marks) can be allowed for diagrams.)

* SRP = Significant Relevant Point – a clear geographical point that is relevant to the question asked.

Remember!

For mark security, always give **more** than the number of SRPs required.

3 (a) Link each letter in Figure 2 with its matching description in the boxes below.

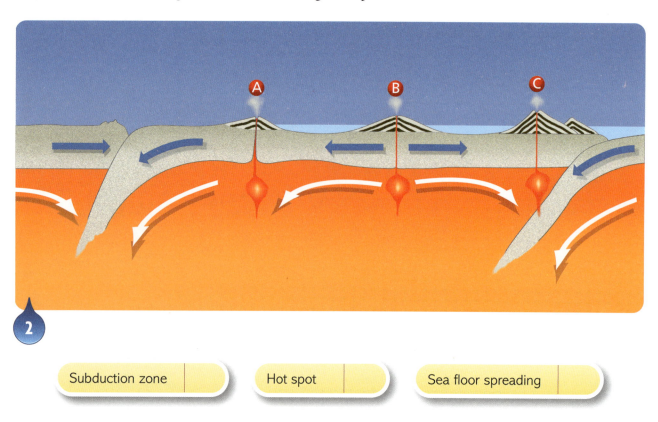

2

Subduction zone

Hot spot

Sea floor spreading

(b) Name one type of rock formed from lava. _____

(c) In the space provided, name and describe two types of material other than lava that are emitted by a volcano.

● Name: _____

● Description: _____

_____

_____

_____

● Name: _____

● Description: _____

_____

_____

_____

4 (a) Match each of the features labelled **A–L** in Figure 3 with the correct named feature in the grid below. One match has been made for you.

(Based on LC Ordinary Level question.)

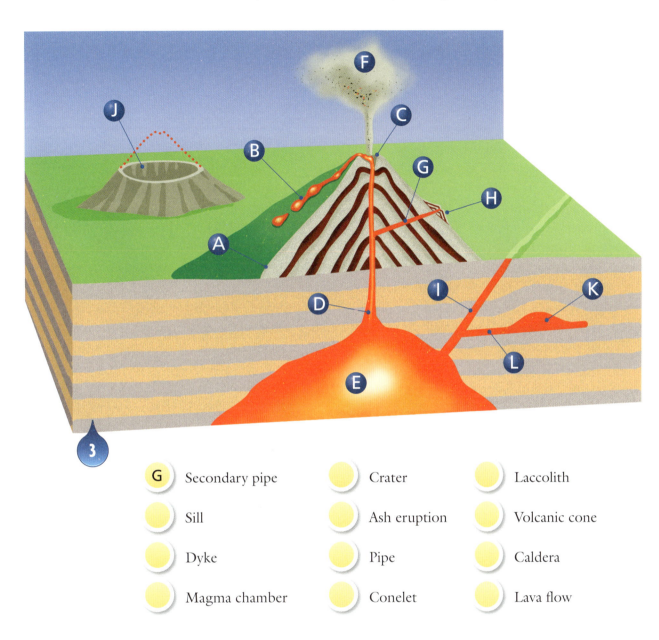

G Secondary pipe	Crater	Laccolith
Sill	Ash eruption	Volcanic cone
Dyke	Pipe	Caldera
Magma chamber	Conelet	Lava flow

(b) Explain what is meant by each of the following terms.

• Volcanic sill: _____

_____

• Laccolith: _____

_____

People and volcanism – a not always disastrous relationship

Humankind's unhappy relationship with volcanic eruptions has long been documented. At the time of the Roman Empire, a man named Pliny the Younger penned an eyewitness account of the eruption of Mount Vesuvius. This volcano (which Romans had assumed to be *extinct*) erupted with deadly effect in August AD 79. Thousands of inhabitants of the nearby towns of Pompeii and Herculaneum were killed instantly by poisonous gases spewed out by the erupting mountain. They (along with their towns) were then buried beneath successive layers of volcanic ash and mud. In 1883, Krakatoa Island in present-day Indonesia exploded with a force equivalent to 26 large atomic bombs. More than 36,000 people died. In 1985, 22,000 people were killed when a *dormant* volcanic mountain called Nevada del Ruiz erupted in Colombia, South America. They died, not directly from the eruption, but from the huge mudflows that ensued when the eruption melted vast quantities of snow and ice that lay on the upper mountain slopes. In April 2010 a volcanic eruption in Iceland killed nobody at all. Nevertheless, it dominated Ireland's media for almost a week. The reason for this was that the eruption emitted a huge plume of fine dust that spread across the skies of Northern Europe. This dust presented deadly danger to jet engines and so virtually closed down European air space for six days.

Volcanism has, however, brought benefits as well as disasters. Heat generated by volcanic *magma* can 'superheat' ground water to above boiling point. This underground heat resource allows people to harvest geothermal energy simply by passing underground circuits of piped water through volcanically affected areas. Geothermal energy can be used to generate electricity or, in towns such as Iceland's Reykjavik, to provide 'free' hot water, much-needed central heating and enjoyable 'hot tubs'.

Tourist industries in many parts of the world have benefited from the effects of local volcanism. One of southern Italy's leading tourist attractions is the town of Pompeii, which has been excavated from its long entombment beneath the volcanic ash and mud of Mount *Vesuvius*. The mountain itself, with its steep-sided cone and dramatic crater, is also a magnet for tourists. The nearby island of *Ischia* has attracted streams of visitors to sample its health-giving and invigorating volcanic spas and hot springs. Volcanic tourist attractions can be found in many other parts of the world. They range from the bleak beauty of Iceland's volcanic landscape to well-publicised novelty attractions such as 'Old Faithful'– the well-visited *geyser* in the USA's Yellowstone National Park.

A good deal of the world's land owes its very existence to volcanism. Iceland is basically a volcanic island that has emerged from the *Mid-Atlantic Ridge* that marks the boundary between the Eurasian and American crustal plates. Closer to home, the Antrim Plateau and the granite-capped Wicklow Mountains are each partly derived from extrusive or *intrusive* volcanic activity. Some volcanic land breaks down into very fertile soil. The presence of so many farms near the slopes of active volcanic mountains such as Vesuvius and Etna bears testimony to this.

Bathing in one of Iceland's many hot pools
Account for the presence of such hot pools in Iceland.

5 (a) Use the news extract on the previous page to complete the grid below.

Some volcanic disasters through the ages				
Volcanic mountain	Year of eruption	Country	Human death toll	Main cause of death
Vesuvius				
Krakatoa				
Nevada del Ruiz				

(b) The answers to the clues below are *terms* or *places* mentioned in the *news extract*. Write the appropriate terms/places to complete the word puzzle.

1 A long undersea ridge that lies between Europe and America
2 Molten underground volcanic matter
3 A volcanic island off southern Italy
4 A volcanic mountain, eruptions from which destroyed Pompeii and Herculaneum
5 An _____ volcano is one that has not erupted in historical time and is not expected to erupt again
6 Volcanic activity or features beneath the earth's surface
7 A _____ volcano is one that has not erupted for a long time but that may erupt again
8 A volcanic spring that intermittently discharges an explosive collection of steam and hot water into the air

(c) Describe two positive effects of volcanism.
Use the news extract to assist you.

_____

_____

_____

_____

_____

_____

_____

_____

6 Effects of Volcanoes

Major flight problems

The ash cloud from a volcano erupting under the Eyjafjallajökull glacier continues to disrupt flights across northern Europe.

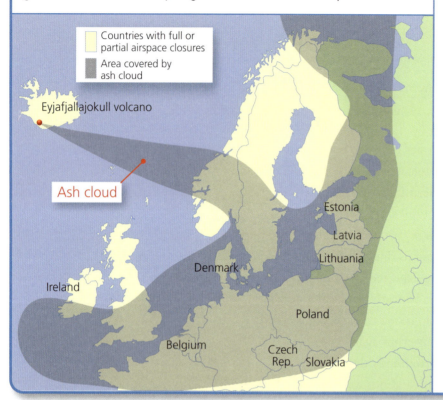

This eruption caused enormous disruption to air travel across western and northern Europe over an initial period of six days in April 2010.

The second phase of the eruption started on 14 April 2010 and resulted in an estimated 250 million cubic metres of ejected ash. The ash cloud rose to a height of approximately 9 kilometres.

By 21 May 2010, the second eruption phase had subsuded to the point that no further lave or ash was being produced.

(a) What approximate height did the volcanic ash cloud rise to?

(b) How many cubic metres of ash were ejected by the volcano?

(c) Name two countries not named on the map which had full or partial airspace closures.

(i) _____ (ii) _____

(d) Explain briefly why volcanic activity occurs in Iceland

_____

_____

_____

(e) Name two problems associated with volcanic activity that have **not** referred to already on this page.

(i) _____ (ii) _____

3 Folding, Doming and Faulting

1 What is *folding?*

_____

_____

2 Draw labelled diagrams of an asymmetrical and an overthrust fold in the boxes below.

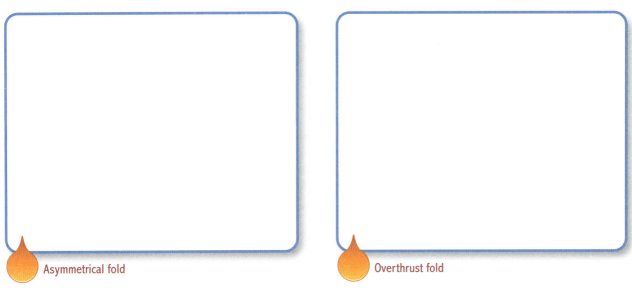

Asymmetrical fold

Overthrust fold

3 The following is a list of four types of fold. Rearrange the list according to the *intensity of pressure* involved in forming the folds. Begin your list with the fold that was formed with the least amount of pressure (1) and end your list with the fold that was formed with the greatest amount of pressure (4).

- Overfold
- Simple fold
- Overthrust fold
- Asymmetrical fold

1 _____

2 _____

3 _____

4 _____

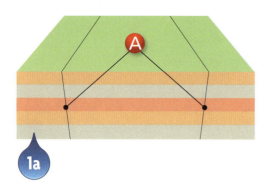

1a

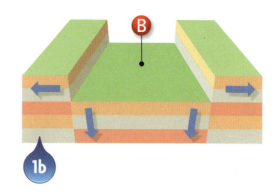

1b

4 (a) Name the features labelled **A** and **B** in Figures 1a and 1b.

A _____

B _____

(b) Explain how feature **B** was formed. Add labels to Figure 1b to illustrate your answer.

_____

_____

_____

_____

_____

_____

_____

_____

_____

_____

5 In the boxes provided, match each structural landform named in **Column X** with the correct letter from **Column Y**.

Column X		Column Y			
1	Rift valley	A	Lateral displacement	1	
2	Block mountains	B	Andes	2	
3	Tear fault	C	East Africa and Scotland	3	
4	Caledonian fold mountains	D	Ox Mountains, Co. Sligo	4	
5	Limb	E	Donegal Mountains	5	
6	Fold mountain range	F	Side of fold	6	

6   The following diagrams show structures of deformation.

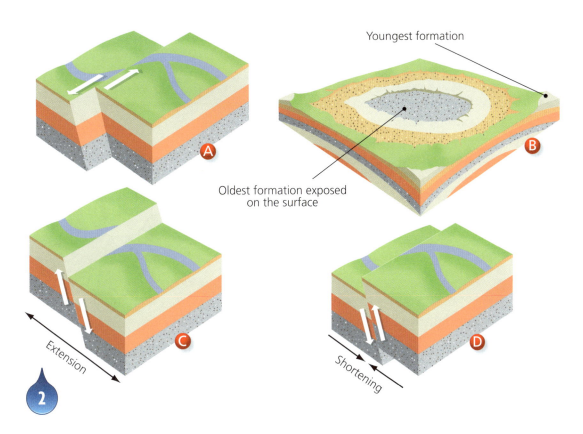

Youngest formation

Oldest formation exposed
on the surface

A

B

Extension

C

Shortening

D

2

(a)   In the boxes provided, match each of the structures listed below with the
correct label **A** to **D** in Figure 2 above.

Normal fault   ◯

Reverse fault   ◯

Doming   ◯

Transverse or tear fault   ◯

(b)   Explain how the structure shown in diagram **B** was formed. _____

_____

_____

_____

_____

_____

_____

Exam training
Answering a thirty-mark question

1 Study the **question** below, which carried 30 marks in a Higher Level Leaving Certificate examination.
2 Study the official **marking scheme** for the question, which is shown below.
3 Then examine the **sample answer** given, which was allocated full marks in the examination.

You can use the experience you gain to help you write 30-mark answers of your own.

The question

 Examine the impact of folding and faulting on the landscape. In your answer refer to one landform in each case.   (30 marks)

The official marking scheme

Folding:
- A landform *named* = **2 marks**
- *Discussion*: 7 (6) significant relevant points (SRPs) at 2 marks each = **14 (12) marks**.
  (A named *example* of the landform can count as one SRP.)

Faulting
- A landform *named* = **2 marks**
- *Discussion*: 7 (6) SRPs @ 2 marks each = **14 (12) marks**.
  (A named example of the landform can count as one SRP.)

(This question did not *require* diagrams, but credit can be given for relevant labelled diagrams.)

Remember!
Try to **exceed the number of SRPs** required by the marking scheme.

A full-mark answer

Landform named and example given ✔

Folding formed the <u>ridge and valley landscape</u> that exists in <u>south Munster</u>. ✔

About 250 million years ago the African and Eurasian plates collided. ✔ This collision created compression (horizontal squeezing) from the south. ✔ The compression folded (crumpled) existing horizontal layers of sedimentary rocks into great east-west folds. ✔ The anticlines or tops of these Armorican folds formed long ridges, ✔ while the synclines or troughs of the folds formed valleys between the ridges. ✔ Today, south Munster consists of east-west limestone valleys and sandstone ridges. ✔ The sandstone was exposed on the ridge surfaces when the overlying limestone was weathered away by rainwater. ✔

2 + 14 = 16

Landform named and example given ✔

Faulting gave rise to <u>rift valleys</u>, such as the great <u>Rift Valley of East Africa</u>. ✔

A long line of hot spots lies beneath the African Rift Valley. ✔ Convection currents of magma rose from these hot spots and created tension (pulling apart) on the earth's crust. ✔ The tension caused parallel faults (splits) to the formed on the earth's crust. ✔ Land between the parallel faults slipped downwards as tension pulled the crust apart. ✔ This process created a 2,400 kilometre-long rift valley to form in a generally north–south direction between the faults. ✔ If this process of rifting continues, the African continent will eventually split apart and a new constructive plate boundary will be created. ✔ Part of the Rift Valley is already under the sea, where it forms the Red Sea and the Gulf of Aden.

2 + 12 = 14

The above full-mark sample answer did not include diagrams. But relevant labelled diagrams such as those below could be used to supplement the answer.

30 / 30

Sandstone Ridge (Anticline)

West — East

Limestone

Limestone Valley (Syncline)

Sandstone

Compression

Rift Valley

Fault Escarpment

tension — tension

Parallel Faults

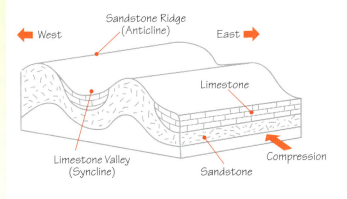

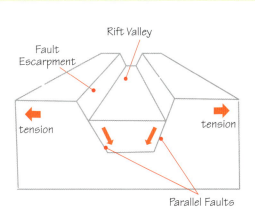

3

4

4 Earthquakes

1 Examine Figure 1 and answer the questions that follow:

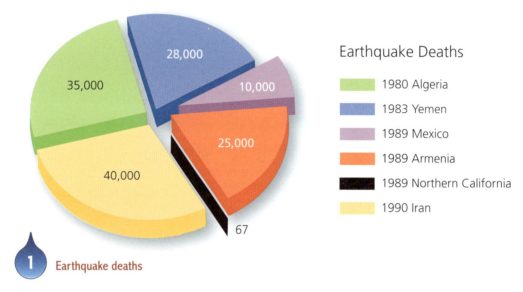

Earthquake Deaths

- 1980 Algeria
- 1983 Yemen
- 1989 Mexico
- 1989 Armenia
- 1989 Northern California
- 1990 Iran

1 Earthquake deaths

(a) Name the year and the country/region with the largest number of earthquake deaths:

Year: _____ Country/region: _____

(b) Name the year and the country/region that experienced 10,000 earthquake deaths.

Year: _____ Country/region: _____

(c) Name the instrument (shown in Figure 2) that is used to measure the strength of earthquakes.

_____

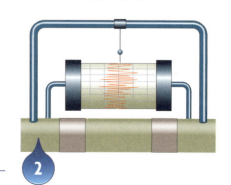

2

(d) Explain briefly why earthquakes occur frequently in northern California.

_____

_____

_____

_____

2 In the boxes provided, match the letter of each term in **Column X** with the number of the correct description in **Column Y.** One match has been made for you.

Column X	
A	Liquefaction
B	Tsunami
C	Transverse fault
D	Seismic gap
E	Tianjin
F	Radon
G	Modified Mercalli scale
H	Richter scale
I	Kashmir
J	Thailand

Column Y	
1	Gas emitted from the earth's crust
2	Endured an earthquake in 2005
3	Destructive sea wave
4	Measures intensity of earthquakes
5	Endured a tsunami on 26 December 2004
6	Where plates move past each other
7	Measures magnitude of earthquakes
8	Period between earthquakes in one area
9	Tremors turn ground into liquid mud
10	Chinese city that endured an earthquake

A	
B	
C	
D	
E	10
F	
G	
H	
I	
J	

3 Explain briefly:

(a) How earthquakes can be predicted. _____

(b) How the effects of earthquakes can be reduced. _____

Case Study:
Hell in Haiti – the earthquake of 2010

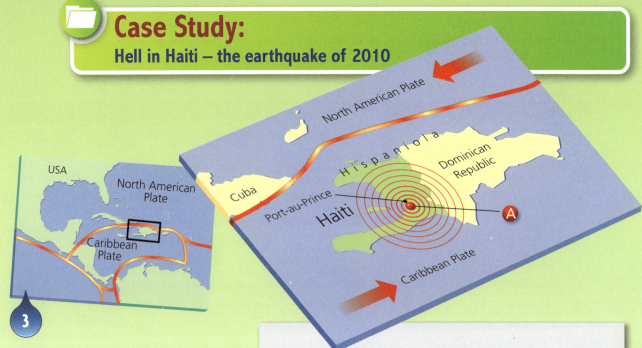

4 Examine the maps (Figure 3) and the news extract (Figure 4) before answering the questions that follow.

Haiti is a small Third World country in the Caribbean Sea. It lies close to a **conservative crustal plate** boundary where the North American Plate moves west relative to the neighbouring Caribbean Plate. A sudden crustal movement along this boundary triggered a devastating earthquake on the afternoon of 12 January 2010.

The tremor lasted for only a minute. But it was a powerful and 'shallow' quake of **7.0 magnitude** whose **focus** was close to the earth's surface. The results of the quake were catastrophic for Haiti. More than 223,000 people died – most of them crushed under poorly constructed buildings that collapsed like houses of cards. The capital city of Port-au-Prince – situated only 15 kilometres from the earthquake epicentre – lost up to 50 per cent of its buildings. The terrible tremor also led to massive mudslides that wiped out entire communities in some of the capital's hillside slums. In all, one million people were left homeless and twice that number were left in urgent need of food and clean water.

Poverty played a major role in Haiti's disaster. The country is the poorest in the western hemisphere. Its buildings, emergency services and social services simply could not cope with a powerful earthquake. Had Haiti been a developed country such as Japan, its death toll would inevitably have been much smaller.

Port-au-Prince after the earthquake.
The floors of multi-storey buildings such as this one collapsed like 'pancakes' one on top of another. The buildings' vertical columns did not contain enough steel to make them earthquake-proof – a symptom of Haiti's poverty.

Using the map (Figure 3)

(a) The place labelled **A** on the map points to the surface directly above the focus of the earthquake.

What name is given to such a place? _____

(b) Explain the meaning of the term 'tear (transverse) faultlines'.

_____

_____

Using the news extract (Figure 4)

(c) Explain briefly but clearly the meaning of each of the terms given below, which are highlighted in the news article.

- Conservative crustal plate: _____

- 7.0 magnitude: _____

- Focus: _____

(d) Describe the principal results of the earthquake and the reasons why those results were so catastrophic.

Principal results	Why results were catastrophic
_____	_____
_____	_____
_____	_____
_____	_____
_____	_____
_____	_____
_____	_____
_____	_____
_____	_____
_____	_____
_____	_____
_____	_____
_____	_____

5 Examine, with reference to actual examples, the measurement and effects of earthquakes. (30 marks)

_____

_____

_____

_____

_____

_____

_____

_____

_____

_____

Leaving Certificate marking scheme

One method of measurement identified = 2 marks
Two effects identified = 2 + 2 marks
Two named examples of earthquakes = 2 + 2 marks

Discussion:
- 5 SRPs relating to measurement = 5 × 2 marks
- 5 SRPs relating to effects = 5 × 2 marks

Total **= 30 marks**

Remember!
It is wise to **exceed the number of SRPs** required by the marking scheme.

_____

_____

_____

_____

_____

_____

_____

_____

_____

_____

_____

_____

_____

_____

_____

_____

1 The rock cycle

Examine the diagram of the rock cycle in Figure 1 and answer the questions that follow.

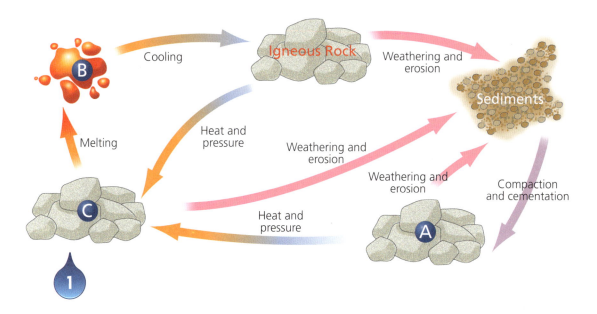

(a) With reference to the labels **A**, **B** and **C** in Figure 1, indicate which letter represents each of the following:

Sedimentary rock ⬤   Metamorphic rock ⬤   Magma ⬤

(b) Use the information in Figure 1 to help you fill in the blank spaces in each of the statements below.

(i) The process of _____ results in the formation of igneous rock.

(ii) The processes of _____ and _____ cause igneous and other rocks to break down into sediment.

(iii) Sediment is changed into rock by the processes of

_____ and _____.

🌐 **2** In the spaces provided below, name one rock type belonging to each of the three rock groups and name one Irish location for each type given.

	Example	Irish location
An igneous rock		
A sedimentary rock		
A metamorphic rock		

3

The photograph shows a well-known **basalt** landscape in Ireland. Select the correct answer from each of the statements below and write it in the space provided:

🌐 (a) This rock is *igneous / sedimentary / metamorphic*. _____

🌐 (b) Basalt cools *deep beneath / close to* the earth's surface. _____

🌐 (c) Basalt cools *quickly / slowly*. _____

🌐 (d) Basalt is a *coarse-grained / fine-grained* rock. _____

🌐 (e) The photograph was taken *in Connemara / at the Giant's Causeway / in the Burren*.

_____

(f) The elevated area in the background of the photograph is the

Antrim-Derry / Donegal _____ Plateau and was formed

less than / more than 100 million years ago.

4 (a) Examine the photographs of different types of rock, below.

In the spaces beneath each photograph:

(i) Name the rock type shown.

(ii) State whether the rock type shown is igneous, sedimentary or metamorphic.

(iii) Name one place in Ireland where the rock type is found.

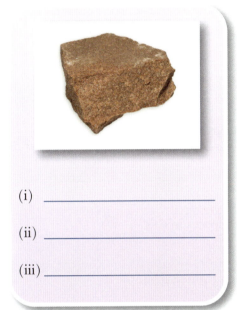

(i) _____

(ii) _____

(iii) _____

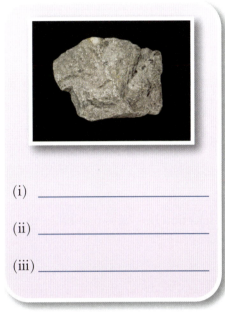

(i) _____

(ii) _____

(iii) _____

(i) _____

(ii) _____

(iii) _____

(b) Describe in detail how igneous rock was formed. _____

_____

_____

_____

_____

_____

_____

_____

_____

_____

_____

_____

5 In the boxes provided, match each term in **Column A** with its appropriate description in **Column B**.

Column A			Column B				
A	Thermal metamorphism		1	Contains mica, feldspar and quartz		A	
B	Regional metamorphism		2	Organic sedimentary rock		B	
C	Marble		3	Caused by heat alone		C	
D	Granite		4	Process by which sedimentary rock is formed		D	
E	Basalt		5	Contained in limestone		E	
F	Lithification		6	Metamorphosed from limestone or chalk		F	
G	Shale		7	Inorganic sedimentary rock		G	
H	Coal		8	Caused by heat and pressure		H	
I	Calcium carbonate		9	An extrusive or volcanic igneous rock		I	

6 Limestone

Select words or terms from the selection box below to fill in the blank spaces in this description of limestone.

Limestone is an _____ sedimentary rock that has been formed from the remains of _____. Limestone in Ireland can be found in places such as the Burren in Co. _____. It was formed beneath a _____ sea about _____ million years ago, at a time when Ireland was situated slightly south of _____. Limestone in Ireland is usually _____ in colour. It contains numerous horizontal layers called _____, which are separated from each other by _____. It also contains vertical cracks called _____, which were formed as the limestone dried out when it was being formed. Limestone is _____, which means that water can pass through it. It is easily weathered by _____ acid, which is contained in rainwater. Limestone sometimes contains the _____ remains of some of the creatures from which it was derived.

Selection Box
citric   bedding planes   the Equator   inorganic   fossilised   Africa   white
sea creatures   permeable   Clare   impermeable   organic   carbonic   vegetation
grikes   350   Wicklow   strata   tropical   dried   joints   400   cold   grey

7 (a) What is meant by each of the following terms?

● Active plate margin _____

_____

_____

● Passive plate margin _____

_____

_____

(b) On the outline map of North America in Figure 2 draw and name an **active plate margin** and a **passive plate margin**.

(c) Describe the principal tectonic processes (activities) that occur in North America's *active plate margin*; and the principal effects of these processes.

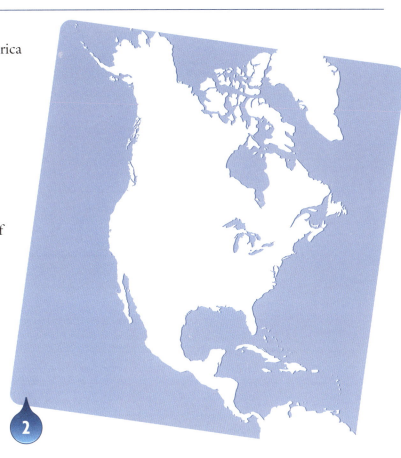

2

● Processes: _____

_____

_____

_____

● Effects: _____

_____

_____

_____

8 Examine how humans interact with the rock cycle in the case of **one** of the following: *mining, quarrying, oil/gas exploration, geothermal energy production.*

Frequently asked question

Sample Higher Level marking scheme

- Interaction identified: 2 marks
- Location identified: 2 marks
- Discussion: 13 SRPs* at 2 marks each

* A second location identified can count as one SRP.

Remember!
Try to **exceed the number of SRPs** required by the marking scheme.

_____

_____

_____

_____

_____

_____

_____

_____

_____

_____

_____

_____

_____

_____

_____

_____

_____

_____

_____

_____

_____

_____

_____

_____

1 In the boxes provided match each item in **Column X** with its associated item in **Column Y**.

Column X	
A	Onion weathering
B	High diurnal temperature range
C	Rock minerals expand
D	Rabbits, foxes and badgers
E	Feldspar turns to clay

Column Y	
1	Hydration
2	Hydrolysis
3	Biological weathering
4	Hot days and cold nights
5	Exfoliation

A	
B	
C	
D	
E	

2 Examine the diagram in Figure 1 and write in the spaces provided the correct answer to each of the following questions.

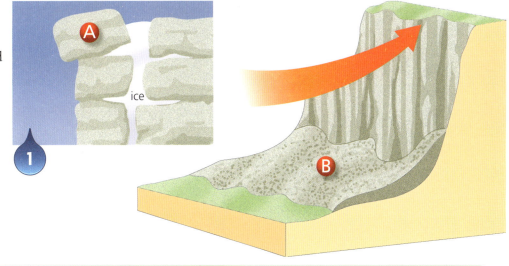

Question	Answer
(a) Identify the weathering agent that is active at **A**.	
(b) Is this weathering agent an example of physical (mechanical) weathering or chemical weathering?	
(c) Which of the following best describes temperatures at **A**? (i) They are always below freezing point (0°C). (ii) They range between above and below freezing point. (iii) They are never below freezing point.	
(d) What name is given to the rock particles (labelled **B**) that gather at the foot of the slope?	

3 Examine the photograph and the diagram in Figure 2.

(a) Identify the types of weathering prevalent in the photograph and in Figure 2.

Photograph: _____

Figure 2: _____

2

(b) Describe in detail the type of weathering illustrated in Figure 2.

_____

_____

_____

_____

_____

_____

_____

_____

_____

_____

_____

_____

_____

_____

_____

4 Revision word puzzle on Chapters 5 and 6

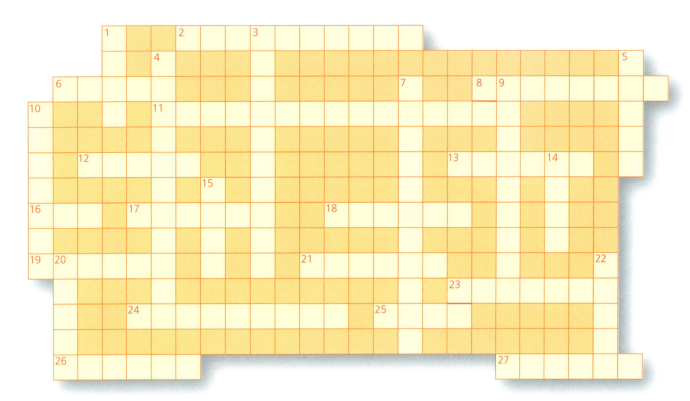

Across

1 Another word for *physical* weathering
6 Inorganic sedimentary rock
8 Country of black marble and famous cats
11 Happens in the Sahel
12 Can be formed from subducted rock that melts
13 Metamorphic rock derived from limestone
16 _ _ _ red sandstone can be found in Munster mountains
17 Metamorphic rock formed from granite
18 Often vertical cracks in limestone
19 Sedimentary rock layers
21 Can be found in granite
23 Metamorphism from heat alone
24 Chemical weathering that affects shale
25 Organic sedimentary rock
26 Expect lots of exfoliation in this desert
27 The _ _ _ _ _ _ is a well-known limestone area in Co. Clare

Down

1 Frost shattering is freeze-_ _ _ _ action
3 Chemical weathering that affects granite
4 Rock group formed from sediments
5 Exfoliation is _ _ _ _ _ weathering
7 Chemical weathering that affects limestone
9 Plutonic
10 Cooled magma forms this rock group
14 Find quartzite on this Great Sugar _ _ _ _ mountain
15 Moving air – an agent of erosion
20 Scree
22 Metamorphic rock derived from shale

How Rock Types Influence Landscapes

1 Features in and near a karst area

In the boxes provided, name each of the items labelled **A** to **P** in Figure 1.
Select your answers from the selection box below.

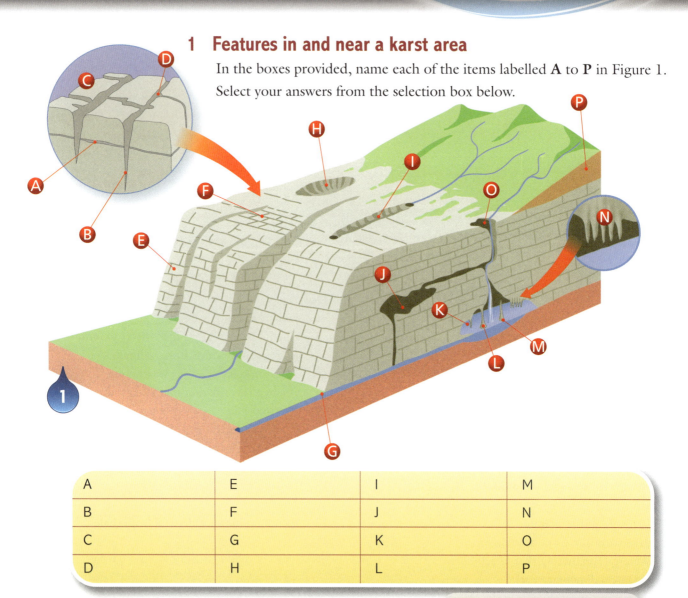

Figure 1

A		E		I		M	
B		F		J		N	
C		G		K		O	
D		H		L		P	

Identify features that were formed on the surface *by drawing circles around them.*

Selection Box

resurgence	cave curtain	stalagmite	clint	bedding plane
pillar	swallow hole	doline	grike	cavern	limestone pavement
limestone cliff	stalactite	area of impermeable rock	dry valley	joint

2 Examine, with reference to an example, the formation of one rock type and how it produces a distinctive landscape.

Frequently asked question

_____

_____

_____

_____

_____

_____

_____

_____

_____

_____

_____

_____

_____

_____

_____

_____

_____

_____

_____

_____

_____

_____

_____

_____

_____

_____

_____

_____

Remember!
Try to **exceed the number of SRPs** required by the marking scheme.

Leaving Certificate marking scheme
- Identify rock type = 2 marks
- Named example (location) = 2 marks
- Formation: 5/6 SRPs @ 2 marks each = 10/12 marks
- Identify landscape = 2 marks
- Named location = 2 marks
- Distinctive landscape: 5/6 SRPs @ 2 marks each = 10/12 marks

3 With reference to the Irish landscape, examine the processes that have influenced the development of any landform in a **karst** region.

Leaving Certificate marking scheme

- Identify the landform: 2 marks
- Name an Irish example: 2 marks
- Name a process: 2 marks
- 12 SRPs @ 2 marks each 24 marks

Total **30 marks**

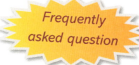

Frequently asked question

A full-mark sample answer

A swallow hole is a funnel-shaped hole in a limestone surface through which rivers disappear underground. An Irish example of a swallow hole is Pollnagcolm in the Burren.

Landform identified: 2 marks

Example: 2 marks

When a river begins to flow over an exposed limestone surface, some of its water percolates down through joints in the limestone. ✔ There is greater downward percolation where a number of joints intersect. ✔

These joints are gradually enlarged by carbonation, which is the chemical weathering of limestone by rainwater. ✔ The rainwater absorbs carbon dioxide as it forms in the atmosphere. ✔ It then becomes a dilute carbonic acid. ✔ Carbonic acid reacts chemically with calcium carbonate in limestone. ✔ It turns the calcium carbonate into calcium bicarbonate. ✔ Because calcium carbonate is soluble, it dissolves in the rainwater and so causes the limestone to be weathered. ✔

Process: 2 marks

The intersecting joints eventually become enlarged enough to form a single downward passage ✔ through which the river can disappear underground. This passage is a swallow hole and it will be enlarged further by the following processes.

- Hydraulic action, which is erosion carried out by the force of the river's moving water. ✔
- Abrasion, which is carried out by pebbles and other 'load' materials carried along by the river. ✔ These materials erode the sides of the swallow hole as they crash against it.

Swallow holes often develop at boundaries between areas of limestone pavement and areas of impermeable rock such as shale. ✔ Rivers that flow over the surfaces of impermeable rock disappear suddenly through swallow holes when they enter the limestone pavement.

30 / 30

Now answer question 3 yourself on the formation of a **cave pillar**. In your answer you may also describe the formation of stalactites and stalagmites, which eventually combine to form cave pillars. Use the Leaving Certificate marking scheme provided on the previous page to help guide your answer.

Try to **exceed** the number of SRPs required by the marking scheme

4 Examine the features **A** and **B** shown in the photograph and the diagram below. In the spaces provided, identify each feature, name an area where that feature might be found and describe briefly how the feature was formed.

cavern

Feature A: _____

Found in: _____

Formation: _____

_____

_____

_____

_____

_____

Feature B: _____

Found in: _____

Formation: _____

_____

_____

_____

_____

_____

5 Indicate which of the following items are **surface landforms** by writing **SL** after them, which are **underground landforms** by writing **UL** after them and which are *processes* by writing **P** after them. One item has been completed for you.

Carbonation	P
Dolines	
Sluggas	
Hydraulic action	
Limestone pavement	

Abrasion	
Stalactite	
Cave	
Karren	
Limestone passage	

8 Mass Movement

1 (a) The photographs labelled **A** to **D** show different types of mass movement.
Match each label **A–D** with the correct description.

Rockfall ⬤   Solifluction ⬤   Debris avalanche ⬤   Avalanche ⬤

(b) Describe briefly any *three factors* that affect mass movement.

(i) _____

_____

(ii) _____

_____

(iii) _____

_____

2 The diagram in Figure 1 shows the speed and water content of mass movement. The labels **A** to **E** refer to different types of mass movement. Examine the position in the diagram of each label and name the type of mass movement that it represents. Choose your answer from the list given in the selection box.

Selection Box

- Mudflow
- Soil creep
- Earthflow
- Rockfall
- Solifluction

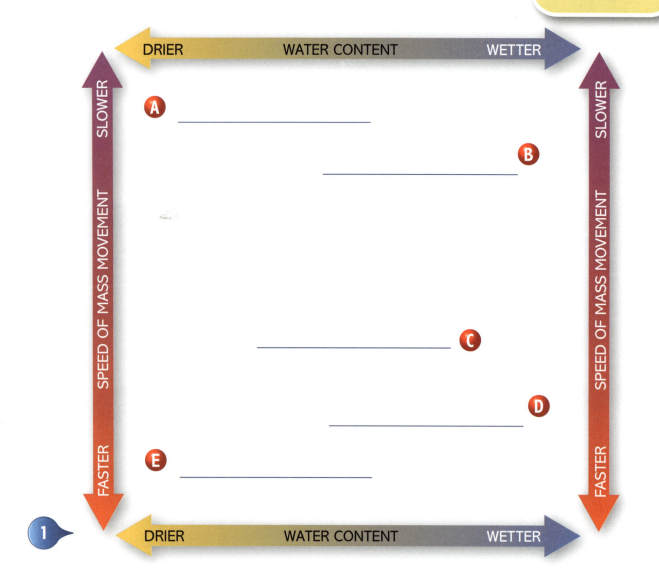

3 Match each of the items in **Column X** with the appropriate item in **Column Y**.

Column X	
A	Soil creep
B	Solifluction
C	Bogburst
D	Rotational slumping
E	Avalanches
F	Scar and lobe

Column Y
Features of earthflows
Often associated with landslides
Occurs often where permafrost exists
Often occur in the Alps
Can occur on the gentlest of slopes
Happened at Derrybrien, Co. Galway in 2003

4   With the aid of a diagram or diagrams, describe *soil creep* **or** *landslides*.
In your answer, you may, if you wish, refer to how people cause or are affected
by the type of mass movement chosen. Refer also to one place in Ireland where
the type of mass movement that you have chosen occurs.   (30 marks)

_____

_____

_____

_____

_____

_____

_____

_____

_____

_____

_____

_____

_____

_____

_____

 For diagrams

5 In the spaces provided, explain briefly the meaning of each of the following terms.

- **Mass wasting** _____

  _____

- **Terracette** _____

  _____

- **Solifluction** _____

  _____

- **Lahar** _____

  _____

- **Bogburst** _____

  _____

6 Word puzzle

Complete this word puzzle on the names of types of mass movement. The clues are given in the diagrams in Figure 2.

very fast

typical speed of mass movement

River Processes, Patterns and Landforms

1   Match each of the terms in **Column X** with the correct description in **Column Y**.

Column X	
A	Abrasion
B	Saltation
C	Waterfall
D	Alluvial fan
E	Oxbow lake

Column Y
Landform created by deposition
Process of erosion
Landform created by erosion and deposition
Process of transportation
Landform created by erosion

2   *Hydraulic action and attrition are two types of fluvial erosion.*
Explain how hydraulic action and attrition work.

●   Hydraulic action: _____

_____

_____

_____

_____

●   Attrition: _____

_____

_____

_____

_____

⊕ **3** Match each landform in **Column X** with the appropriate description in **Column Y**.

Column X	
A	Delta
B	Soil creep
C	Gorge
D	Rift valley
E	Clint

Column Y
Structural landform
Weathering landform
Erosional landform
Depositional landform
Mass movement

4 Examine the diagram in Figure 1.

In the spaces provided in the table below:

(a) Identify each of the landforms/features labelled **A** to **F**.

(b) State whether each landform is a feature of erosion, deposition or both erosion and deposition.

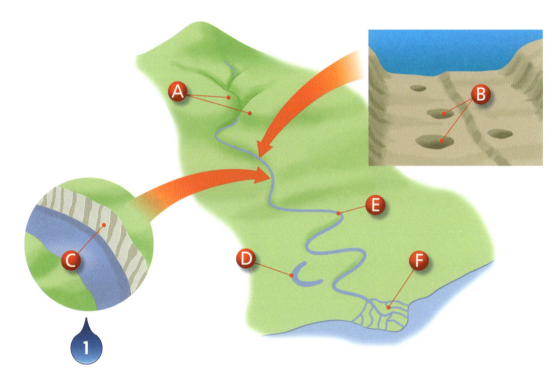

	Name of Landform	Erosion, deposition or both
A		
B		
C		
D		
E		
F		

5 In the spaces provided, write a brief but clear explanation of each of these geographical terms:

(a) **Abrasion** _____

_____

(b) **Hydraulic action** _____

_____

(c) **River discharge** _____

_____

(d) **Saltation** _____

_____

(e) **Drainage system** _____

_____

(f) **River course** _____

_____

(g) **Lateral erosion** _____

_____

(h) **Headward erosion** _____

_____

(i) **Bank caving** _____

_____

(j) **Alluvial soil** _____

_____

(k) **Mort lake** _____

_____

(l) **Distributary** _____

_____

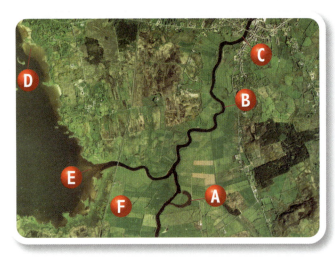

🌐 6 (a) Study the photograph. Indicate with an **X** in the correct box whether the statement that follows is *true* or *false*. 'The river in the photograph is in its upper course and is mainly eroding.'

True ⬤   False ⬤

🌐 (b) What name is given to the feature labelled **A** on the photograph?

_____

(c) Identify the landform labelled **B** on the photograph. _____

(d) Identify each of the following features by their label on the photograph:

Flood plain ⬤   Settlement with bridge point ⬤

River mouth ⬤   Fluvial or marine deposition ⬤

7 Examine the diagram of a river meander in Figure 2.
Identify each of the following by its label (**A–E**) on the diagram.

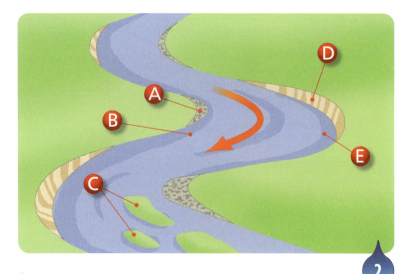

2

- Braiding ⬤

- Slip-off slope/point bar ⬤

- River cliff ⬤

- Place of maximum river speed ⬤

- Place of minimum river speed ⬤

8 Examine, with the aid of a labelled diagram or diagrams, the processes that have led to the formation of one Irish landform of your choice. (30 marks)

Frequently asked question

_____
_____
_____
_____
_____
_____
_____
_____
_____
_____
_____
_____
_____
_____
_____
_____
_____
_____
_____
_____
_____
_____
_____
_____

Note
- This question is mainly about **processes**.
- In your answer you must mention an **Irish example**.
- You must include a **diagram** or **diagrams** in your answer.

Marking scheme

Landform (feature) named:	= 2 marks
One process named:	= 2 marks
One Irish example named:	= 2 marks
Labelled diagram:	= 4 marks (graded)
Examination/development: 10 SRPs @ 2 marks each	= 20 marks
Total	**= 30 marks**

Try to **exceed the number of SRPs** required by the marking scheme.

9 Name each of the **drainage patterns** labelled **A** to **D** in the diagrams in Figure 3.

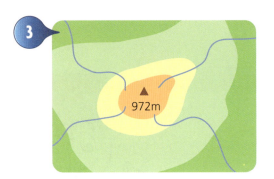

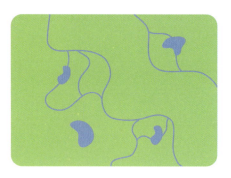

A _____

B _____

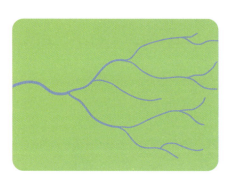

C _____

D _____

10 (a) Identify and give one example of the type of delta shown in Figure 4.

Type of delta: _____   Example: _____

(b) Name the feature labelled **X** in Figure 4.

_____

(c) Explain briefly how the feature in Figure 4 was formed.

_____

_____

_____

_____

11 Examine how human processes can have an impact on the operation of **one** of the following:

- Mass movement process
- River processes
- Coastal processes

Frequently asked Higher and Ordinary Level question

_____

_____

_____

_____

_____

_____

_____

_____

_____

_____

_____

_____

_____

_____

_____

_____

_____

_____

_____

_____

_____

Higher Level marking scheme

- Human process identified: 2 marks
- Example named: 2 marks
- Reference to a natural process: 2 marks
- Examination/development:
  12 SRPs @ 2 marks each = 24 marks

Total = 30 marks

10 Isostasy, Rivers and Landscape Development

1 Indicate by ticking the correct box whether each of the following statements is true or false.

	True	False
(a) The asthenosphere of the earth is made up of soft liquid rock	◯	◯
(b) The theory of isostasy states that the earth's asthenosphere 'floats' on the earth's lithosphere	◯	◯
(c) Isostatic equilibrium occurs when there is a 'balance' between the crust and the upper mantle on which it 'floats'	◯	◯
(d) Isostatic uplift happened following the melting of the ice sheets of the last great Ice Age	◯	◯
(e) The base level of a river is the lowest level to which a river can wear its bed	◯	◯

2 Use the boxes provided to match each of the terms in **Column X** with the correct statement in **Column Y**.

Column X		Column Y			
A	Knickpoint	1	Causes part of the lithosphere to 'float' higher on the asthenosphere	A	
B	Graded river	2	Represents a balance between fluvial erosion and deposition	B	
C	Incised meander	3	Has experienced rejuvenation	C	
D	Plateau	4	Occurs where an older and a newer (rejuvenated) river profile meet	D	
E	Isostatic uplift	5	High and generally flat land	E	
F	Peneplain	6	A clear but simplified view of reality	F	
G	River Nore	7	Low and generally flat land	G	
H	Geographical model	8	Is formed when a river maintains its winding path during rejuvenation	H	

3   Examine the diagram in Figure 1.

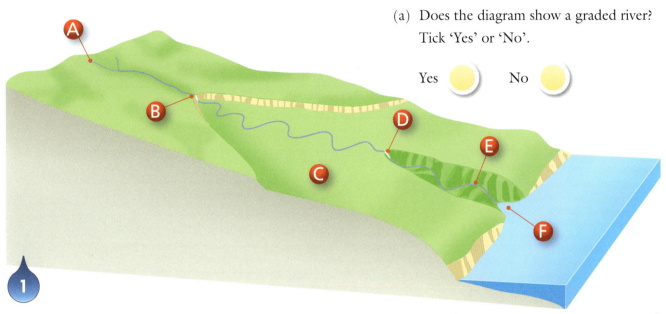

1

(a) Does the diagram show a graded river?
Tick 'Yes' or 'No'.

Yes ⬤   No ⬤

	Base level
	More recently formed knickpoint
	Rejuvenated terrace
	Source of river
	Incised meander
	Older knickpoint

(b) Match each of the features labelled **A** to **F** on Figure 1 with the appropriate feature given in the grid provided.

(c) In the spaces provided, describe fully how each of the features labelled **C** and **E** were formed.

● Feature C: _____

_____

_____

_____

_____

● Feature E: _____

_____

_____

_____

_____

4 Referring to an Irish example, discuss the statement that '*landscape develops in a cyclical manner*'.   (30 marks)

_____

_____

_____

_____

_____

_____

_____

_____

_____

_____

_____

_____

_____

_____

_____

_____

_____

_____

_____

_____

_____

_____

_____

_____

_____

Marking scheme

- Identify at least three steps in the cyclical development of landscape: 2 marks each   = 6 marks
- Mention one Irish example: = 2 marks
- Discussion/development: 11 SRPs* @ 2 marks each   = 22 marks

Total: **= 30 marks**

* Try to **exceed the number of SRPs** required by the marking scheme.

5 All about rivers!

A revision word puzzle on Chapters 9 and 10.

The number following each clue refers to the page number in the textbook where the answer can be found.

Across

1 Tree-like river pattern (95)
4 The theory that says the lithosphere floats on the upper mantle (102)
6 This level is the lowest to which a river can wear its bed (103)
7 Place where two or more rivers meet (85)
8 Tributary of French river in 2 Down (97)
10 Tidal part of a river (85)
13 Type of erosion that causes a river load to break down (82)
15 Process by which breaking air bubbles contribute to erosion (93)
17 Type of fluvial erosion *and* transportation (82 and 83)
19 River in 2 Down rises in these mountains (97)
23 Lower course or senile river (86)
24 May be the site of a waterfall in a rejuvenated river (103)
25 Very steep-sided and narrow valley (87)
26 This pool might be found at the foot of a waterfall (89)
27 This drainage pattern sounds crazy (97)

Down

1 Volume of water in a river (81)
2 Lyon and Arles are on this French river (98)
3 Sideward erosion (86)
5 Bouncing type of river transportation (83)
9 These spurs may be found in a 'young' river valley (87)
11 Triangular-shaped delta (94)
12 Wide river loops (90)
14 A dragging type of river transportation (83)
16 Irish river with estuarine delta (94)
18 A middle-course river valley is sometimes called this (86)
20 _____ caving causes river cliffs to form on the outsides of meanders (90)
21 Large African river with type of delta in 11 Down (94)
22 The part of a river that touches the sea (85)

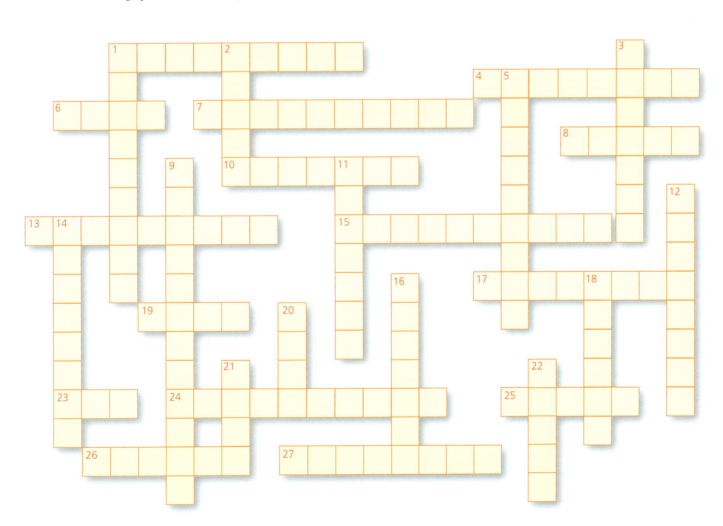

1 Match each of the *marine processes* named in **Column A** with the correct description in **Column B**.

Column A			Column B				
A	Wave refraction		1	When water dissolves rock		A	
B	Longshore drift		2	How the force of water erodes		B	
C	Solution		3	The zigzag movement of material along the shore		C	
D	Abrasion		4	Erosion by trapped and released air		D	
E	Attrition		5	Erosion of the waves' load		E	
F	Compression		6	Causes erosion on headlands and deposition in bays		F	
G	Hydraulic action		7	Erosion by the waves' load		G	

2 Write **one** sentence to describe the **difference** between the two items in each pair below.

(a) **Shore** and **coast** _____

_____

(b) **Destructive wave** and **constructive wave** _____

_____

(c) **Backwash** and **undertow** _____

_____

(d) **Ridge** and **runnel** _____

_____

(e) **Bar** and **tombolo** _____

_____

3 In the space below, draw a **sketch map** of the Ordnance Survey (OS) map extract in Figure 1. Draw your sketch to the same scale as the original map. On your sketch show and name each of the following.

- The coast.
- The shore (use pencil to shade the shore).
- Three landforms of marine erosion.
- Three landforms of marine deposition.
- Two features of human geography that indicate the economic benefit of coastal areas or landforms.

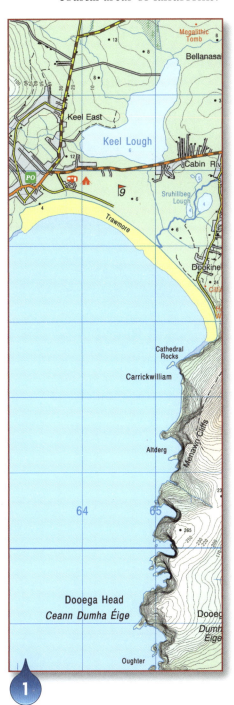

Draw your sketch on this side of the page

4

Examine the photographs above.

(a) Are the sea waves shown constructive waves or destructive waves? _____

    How do you know? _____

    _____

    _____

(b) Name each of the coastal features labelled **A** to **D** and the type of vegetation labelled **E**.

    A   _____   B   _____

    C   _____   D   _____

    E   _____

(c) Briefly explain the **process** or **processes** that led to the formation of the feature labelled **B** in the photograph.

    _____

    _____

    _____

    _____

5 (a) Complete the crossword puzzle by identifying each of the features labelled **A** to **P** on the diagram.

(b) In the **grid** beside the crossword puzzle indicate whether each of the features **A** to **P** is a feature of coastal erosion or a feature of coastal deposition. Write **E** for features of erosion and **D** for features of deposition.

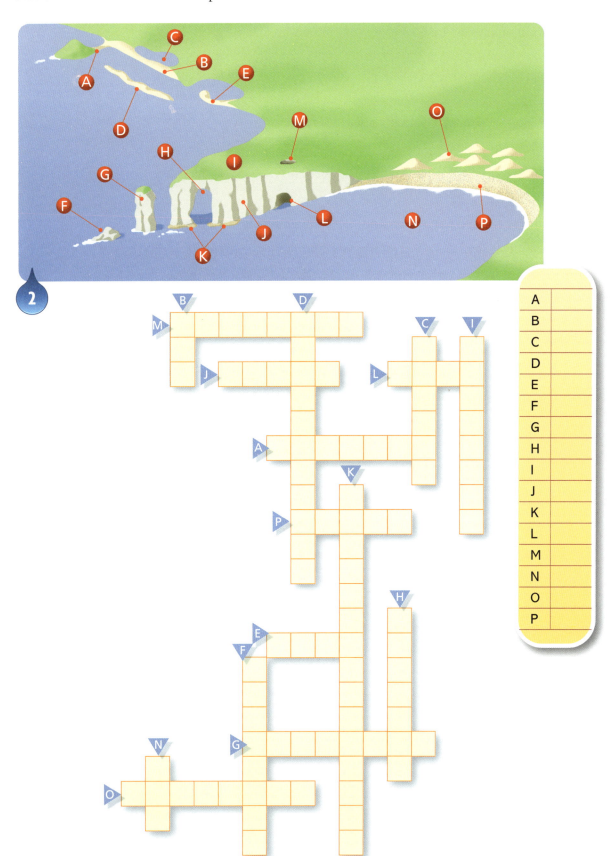

Higher Level question, marking scheme and sample answer

🌐 **6** Examine, with the aid of a labelled diagram or diagrams, the processes that have led to the formation of any one Irish landform of your choice.

Marking scheme

- Landform identified: = 2 marks
- One process named: = 2 marks
- One Irish example: = 2 marks
- Labelled diagram(s) (graded from 1 mark to 6 marks): = 6 marks
- Examination/development: 9 SRPs @ 2 marks each = 18 marks

Total = **30 marks**

Landform, process and Irish example given 3 x 2 = 6 marks

A beach ✓² such as Dollymount Strand ✓² in Dublin is the landform that I have chosen.

Most beaches are formed by constructive wave deposition ✓² on gently sloping coastlines.

Constructive waves have powerful swashes that carry materials up the wide shore. These waves then spread out, so that much of their water soaks into the sandy or pebbly ground. ✓ This means that the backwash of each wave will be smaller and weaker than the swash and so will be less able to remove materials down the shore. ✓ This leads to the formation of a beach because it causes material to be deposited on rather than eroded from the shore. ✓ It also causes material to be stratified or sorted on the beach; with larger stones being left on the backshore (top of the beach), while finer sand is concentrated on the foreshore. ✓

Longshore drift can also contribute to beach formation. ✓ Pebbles and sand carried along the shore by longshore drift will be deposited as beach material where longshore drift is interrupted. ✓ This happens on sheltered parts of the shore where the coastline changes direction. ✓

Wave refraction can cause 'pocket beaches' to form in bays. ✓ As oncoming waves refract or bend around headlands, their power is concentrated around the headlands and dissipated in the bays. The reduced energy of such dissipated waves causes beach material to be deposited in the bays. ✓

Storm beaches occur at the very backs of some beaches. These heaps of large stones are deposited during storms when sea waves are at their most powerful. ✓ Sea deposition may also cause gravely ridges called berms, or gently sloping sandy ridges to form on beaches. ✓ The depressions that separate sandy ridges are known as runnels (see the diagram). ✓

Examination and development: 18 marks

Labelled diagram: 6/6

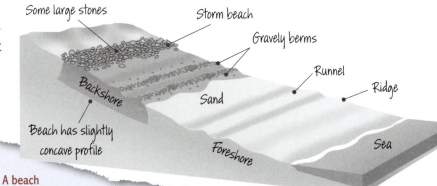

Some large stones — Storm beach — Gravely berms — Runnel — Ridge
Backshore — Sand — Foreshore — Sea
Beach has slightly concave profile

7

Write your own answer to question 6.
Use the same marking scheme to guide you,
but use a *different landform* from the one
used in the sample answer on page 58.

Diagram(s)

Higher Level question with marking scheme

8 Discuss how *one* of the following could impact on the landscape.

- Deforestation
- Coastal management
- Flood control

Marking scheme

- One impact identified: = 2 marks
- Examination/discussion: 14 SRPs @ 2 marks each = 28 marks

Total = 30 marks

(Credit given for up to three examples.)

_____

_____

_____

_____

_____

_____

_____

_____

_____

_____

_____

_____

_____

_____

_____

_____

_____

_____

_____

_____

_____

_____

12 Glacial Processes, Patterns and Landforms

⊕ **1** In the spaces provided, match each of the named landforms in **Column X** with the appropriate description in **Column Y**.

Column X			Column Y				
A	Meander		1	Marine action		A	
B	Moraine		2	Weathering		B	
C	Sand spit		3	Fluvial action		C	
D	Scree		4	Glacial action		D	

2 In relation to each of the items listed below, tick **one** correct box from **Column A** and **one** correct box from **Column B**.

	Column A			Column B		
	Glaciated	Coastal	Fluvial	Process	Erosional landform	Depositional landform
Arête	○	○	○	○	○	○
Blowhole	○	○	○	○	○	○
Compression	○	○	○	○	○	○
Drumlin	○	○	○	○	○	○
Erratic	○	○	○	○	○	○
Headland	○	○	○	○	○	○
Longshore drift	○	○	○	○	○	○
Plucking	○	○	○	○	○	○
Sand spit	○	○	○	○	○	○
Tarn	○	○	○	○	○	○
Waterfall	○	○	○	○	○	○

⊕ **3** Match each of the surface processes in **Column A** with the correct example in **Column B**.

Column A	
A	Erosional
B	Structural
C	Mass movement
D	Depositional

Column B	
1	Soil creep
2	Fold mountain
3	Pothole
4	Esker

A	
B	
C	
D	

4 Name and describe the glacial processes that happen at each of the places labelled **A** and **B** in Figure 1.

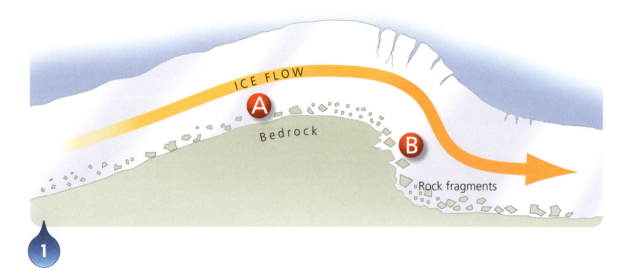

1

Ⓐ _____

_____

_____

_____

_____

_____

Ⓑ _____

_____

_____

_____

_____

_____

5 (a) Indicate in the box below which of the following landforms is illustrated by each of the places labelled **A**, **B** and **C** in the photograph and at **L 992 655** and **M 002 648** on the map fragment (Figure 2).

- A corrie or cirque
- An arête
- A pyramidal peak
- A tarn

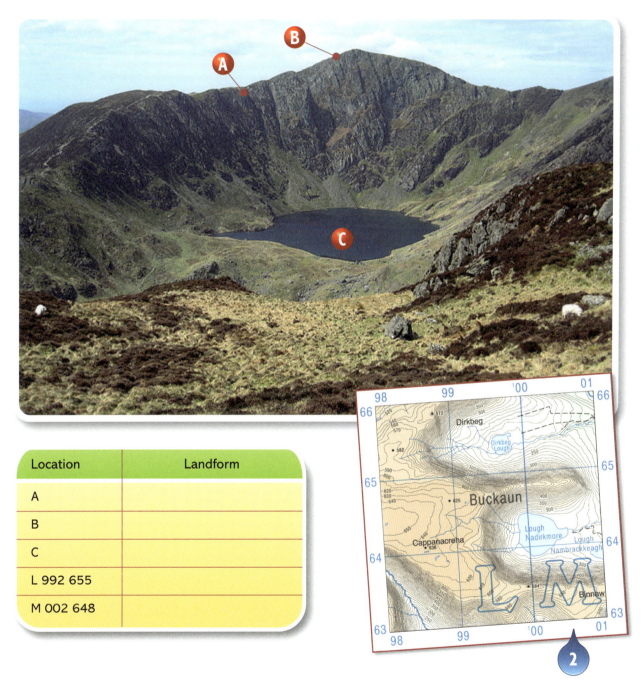

Location	Landform
A	
B	
C	
L 992 655	
M 002 648	

(b) Describe briefly the formation of the landform labelled **C** in the photograph.

_____

_____

_____

_____

Frequently asked
Leaving Certificate
Higher Level question

6 With the aid of a labelled diagram or diagrams, examine the *processes* that have led to the formation of any one landform* of your choice.

* In this case, examine a **glacial** landform.

_____

_____

_____

_____

_____

_____

_____

_____

_____

_____

_____

_____

_____

_____

_____

_____

_____

_____

_____

_____

_____

Leaving Certificate marking scheme

- Landform identified: = 2 marks
- One process named: = 2 marks
- One Irish example: = 2 marks
- Labelled diagram(s): = 6 marks (graded 1 to 6)
- Examination/development: 9 SRPs* @ 2 marks each = 18 marks

  Total = **30 marks**

* Try to **exceed the number of SRPs** required by the marking scheme.

7 The diagram in Figure 3 shows landforms of glacial erosion and deposition, labelled **A** to **J**. Write the letters **A** to **J** in their correct places next to the features listed in the table below. Also indicate, with a tick in the correct column, whether each landform is formed by erosion or by deposition.

Glacial landforms **3**

Feature	Letter	Erosion	Deposition
Drumlin			
Esker			
Hanging valley			
Lateral moraine			
Medial moraine			
Outwash plain			
Pyramidal peak			
Cirque			
Terminal moraine			
Truncated spur			

Congratulations!
You have completed the Physical Geography section of your course.
Now have fun with this revision word puzzle, which covers all aspects of physical geography.

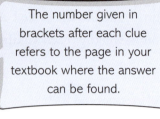

The number given in brackets after each clue refers to the page in your textbook where the answer can be found.

Down

A Exfoliation (60)
B Limestone contains lots of this (51)
C Island of the Mid-Atlantic Ridge (8)
D Limestone cave feature in the picture (70)
E Horizontal layers in sedimentary rock (51)

Across

1 Type of glacial lake in the picture (127)
2 Pipe of volcanic mountain (14)
3 Might be found in limestone (51)
4 Boundary where plates collide (5)
5 Between grikes in limestone pavement (65)
6 Type of lake in the picture (93)
7 Depositional ridge at side of old river (92)
8 Not a simple/symmetrical fold (29)
9 Distance of open sea over which a wave moves (107)
10 Pulverised rock in volcanic eruption (16)
11 Another word for pyroclasts (16)
12 Volcanic mud flow (16)
13 When a stalactite and a stalagmite join together (70)
14 Crustal plate near South America (6)
15 Pacific _____ of Fire (13)
16 _____- *thaw action* – a form of weathering (59)
17 Intrusive volcanic feature – small and dome-shaped (22)
18 Knife-edged ridge between cirques (126)
19 'Land of Fjords' (129)
20 Type of red sandstone found on Munster mountains (31)
21 Winding ridge – landform of fluvio-glacial deposition (134)
22 Famous Co. Antrim basalt site (19)
23 Moraine at side of glacier (130)
24 Feature of river deposition in the picture (94)
25 Glacial process of erosion (125)
26 Where a river begins (85)
27 Where a river ends (85)
28 These glacial deposits may form swarms (133)
29 Igneous rock of Antrim Plateau (19)
30 Instrument used to measure earthquakes (38)
31 Scale used to measure earthquakes – not Richter (38)
32 Large depression in karst area (67)
33 Talus (59)
34 This type of valley can be found in Scotland and Africa (34)
35 Small coastal hill of sand (115)
36 Steep-sided limestone hill in China – sounds musical (71)
37 Feature of both karst and coastal scenery (110)
38 Metamorphosed limestone (53)
39 Basin-shaped hollow formed by glacial erosion (126)
40 This north island in Dublin sounds like an animal (118)
41 Centre of the earth (1)
42 Volcanic mountain in Sicily (17)
43 Volcanic emission that was once magma (14)
44 Rocky outcrop on summit of granite mountain (72)
45 Horizontal, underground sheet of igneous rock (22)
46 A fault that is *transverse* (33)
47 The Burren is an example of such a region (64)
48 This coastal feature could be *baymouth* or *offshore* (116/117)
49 Ireland's most common sedimentary rock (51)

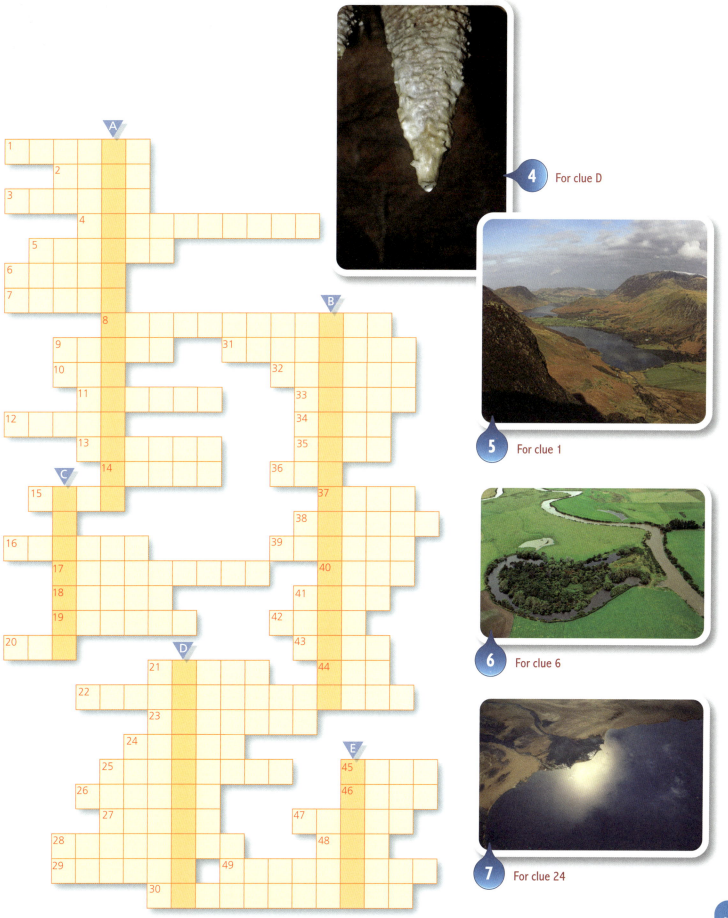

4 For clue D

5 For clue 1

6 For clue 6

7 For clue 24

1. Examine the OS map of the Carlow Area on page 75.

   The scale of the map, expressed as a representative fraction (RF),

   is _____. This means that one _____ on

   the map represents _____ on the ground. Each grid

   square on the map represents _____ square _____.

   Note:

   Questions 1 to 7 are all based on the OS map of the Carlow area on page 75.

2. Examine the OS map of the Carlow area.
   (a) What direction is it from the railway station
   at Carlow to the highest point shown on the map? _____

   (b) In which general direction does the railway line shown on the map run?

   _____

3. Examine the Carlow area map. Circle the correct option in each of the statements below.

   (a) A principal feature located at S 74 77 is *Rathnapish / Pollerton Big /*

   an industrial estate / a college.

   (b) The feature at S 713 791 is *a link road / a spot height / part of a county boundary /*

   a church and crosses.

   (c) The antiquity at S 675 778 is *a burial ground / religious feature / defence feature.*

   (d) The railway station in Carlow is located at *S 771 727 / S 722 771 / S 727 771.*

4. Using the Carlow area map, give a six-figure grid reference for each of the following:
   - The highest point on the map: _____
   - The garda station in Carlow town: _____

5 **Measuring distance and area** using the Carlow area map.
Circle the correct option in each of the following statements.

(a) The shortest distance between the highest point on the map and the

railway station at Carlow is *5.5km / 6.5km / 7.5km / 8.5km.*

(b) The length of the part of the R448 that appears on the map is

7.5km / 8.25km / 9.75km / 10.75km.

(c) The area represented by the map is *90km² / 100km² / 110km² / 120 km².*

(d) The area to the east of the R448 roadway is approximately

20km² / 22km² / 24km² / 26km².

6 **Recognising patterns** on the Carlow area map.
Circle the correct option in each of the following statements.

(a) The type of slope at S 67 73 is *concave / convex / stepped / even.*

(b) The type of slope at S 68 74 is *concave / convex / stepped.*

(c) The settlement pattern at S 74 77 is mainly *dispersed / nucleated / ribboned / absent.*

(d) The settlement pattern at S 71 73 is mainly *dispersed / nucleated / linear / absent.*

(e) The drainage pattern at S 73 71 is *dentritic / trellised / radial / deranged.*

7 Examine the Carlow area map.
In the boxes below, link each of the features listed in **Column A** with its
matching location in **Column B**.

Column A			Column B				
A	S 740 768		1	Road junction		A	
B	S 746 786		2	Post office		B	
C	S 705 770		3	Industrial estate		C	
D	S 685 736		4	Ring fort		D	
E	S 727 765		5	18-hole golf course		E	

8 Feature and symbol recognition

Match each feature or symbol labelled **A** to **U** on the map fragments in
Figure 1 with the correct feature given on the list below Write each letter-
label in the box opposite its match on the list.

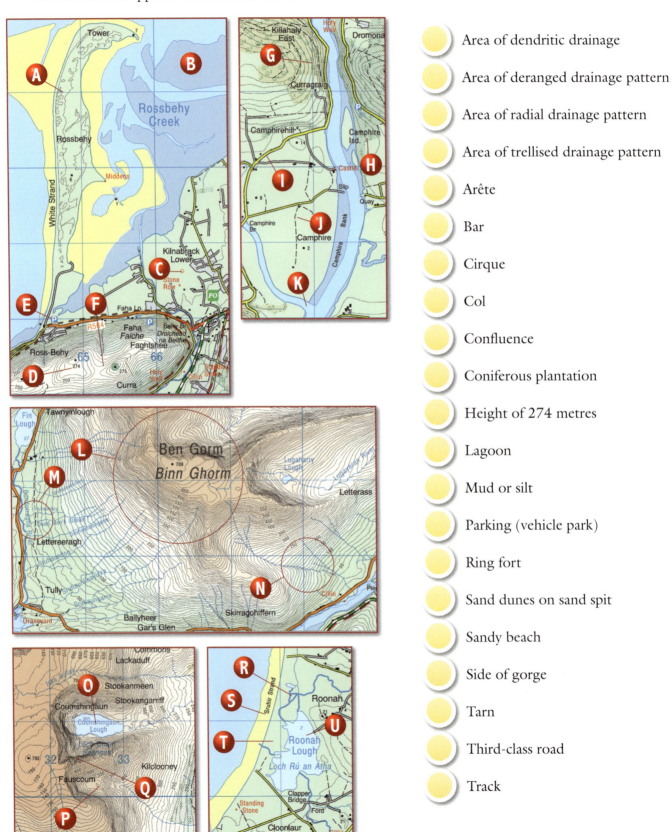

- Area of dendritic drainage
- Area of deranged drainage pattern
- Area of radial drainage pattern
- Area of trellised drainage pattern
- Arête
- Bar
- Cirque
- Col
- Confluence
- Coniferous plantation
- Height of 274 metres
- Lagoon
- Mud or silt
- Parking (vehicle park)
- Ring fort
- Sand dunes on sand spit
- Sandy beach
- Side of gorge
- Tarn
- Third-class road
- Track

1 A selection of OS map fragments

9 Cross-sections (profiles)

Examine the OS map extract in Figure 2 below. Examine also the profile in Figure 3 that was drawn along the trail marked in blue on the map. Answer the questions that follow.

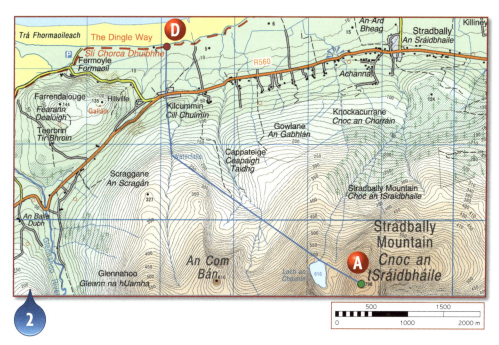

2

3

Actual distance of trail	5,200m
Minimum height on trail	0m
Maximum height on trail	798m

What is the height above sea level at **A**, the start of the trail?	
Identify the glacial landform at **B**	
Name the road at **C**	
Identify a tourist attraction at **D**	

Higher Level question, marking scheme and sample answer

10 With reference to the map in Figure 4, examine three reasons for the development of Cashel. **(30 marks)**

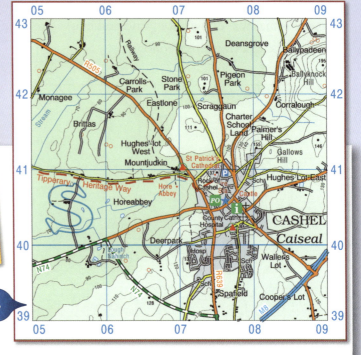

4

Marking scheme

Three reasons @ 10 marks each.
Each 10 marks to be allocated as follows:

- Reason stated = 2 marks
- Accurate map reference = 2 marks
- Three SRPs @ 2 marks each = 6 marks

Note: the red ticks are for the reasons and map references; the blue ticks indicate the SRPs.

Historic <u>defence and ecclesiastical</u> factors probably played a part in the early development of Cashel. ✔ Evidence of this includes the castle at S 077 406 and Hore Abbey at S 069 408. ✔ The castle suggests that Cashel may have been an Anglo-Norman defence settlement during the Middle Ages. ✔ It may have provided protection for local townspeople in times of war or civil unrest. ✔ It is probable that Hore Abbey provided local people with social as well as spiritual services. Such services might have included education for the young, medical care for the sick and alms for the poor. ✔

10/10

Cashel also developed as a <u>nodal point</u> where several roads converge. ✔ These roads include national primary roads such as the N74 and regional roads such as the R505. ✔ Where roads converge, people meet; and where people meet, business and service premises tend to thrive. ✔ Service premises shown on the map include two churches and a garda station at S 076 406. ✔ Cashel probably also developed as a farmer market town for its surrounding low-lying land. Converging roads would then have facilitated the movement of cattle and farm produce to and from fairs in the town. ✔

10/10

The presence of a range of <u>tertiary activities</u> contributed to the development of Cashel. ✔ The map shows the presence in the town of two schools, a county hospital at S 074 404 and a hospital at S073 399. ✔ The presence of a tourist information centre (though one with restricted opening) and of an independent holiday hostel suggests that tourism plays a part in the town's development. ✔ Antiquities such as St Patrick's Cathedral, the castle and Hore Abbey may all attract tourists. ✔ Roads such as the N74 and R505 allow tourists access to the town from many different directions. ✔

10/10

30/30

11 With reference to the map in Figure 5, examine three reasons for the development over time of the town on Mullingar.

Adopt the same **marking scheme** that was used in question 10. Try to **exceed the number of SRPs** required by the marking scheme.

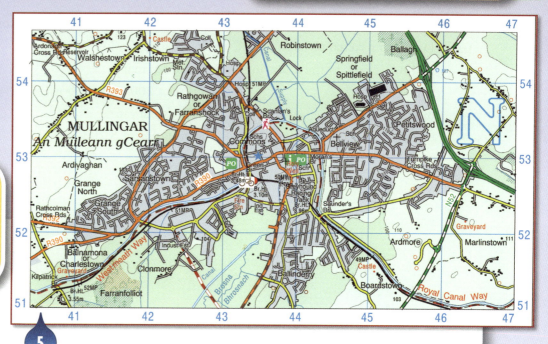

5

12 In the space below, draw a **sketch map*** of the **Carlow area map** on the facing page. Draw your sketch to half the scale of the existing Carlow area map. Show and name each of the following on your sketch map:

- the R448 road
- a motorway
- a county boundary
- land over 200 metres above sea level
- an industrial estate
- the antiquity at S 703 719

* Draw all four sides of the sketch accurately.

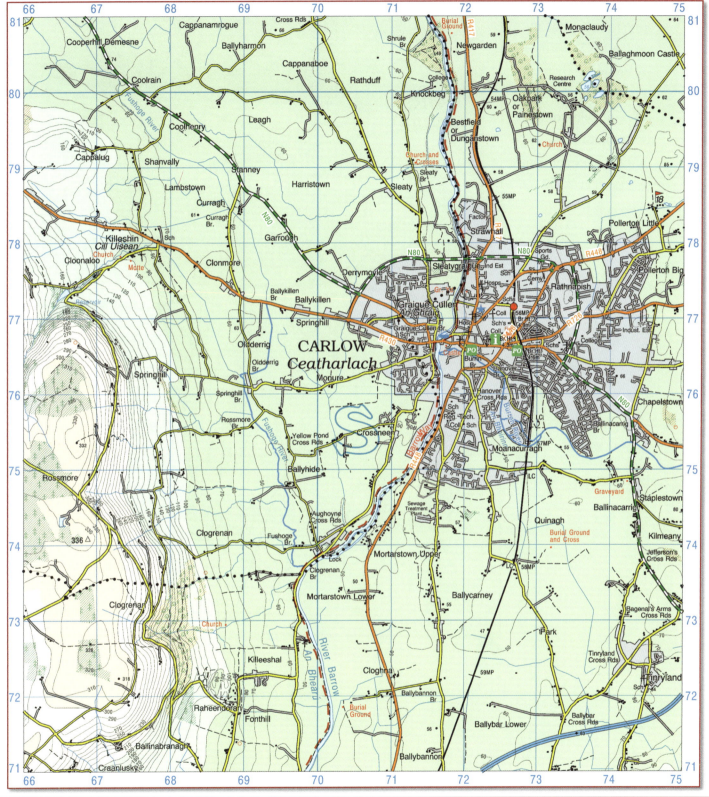

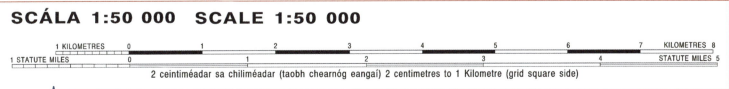

13 Examine the OS map of part of Cork City in Figure 7. With reference to that map, comment on the suitability of the location of the industrial estate that is shown at W 67 69.

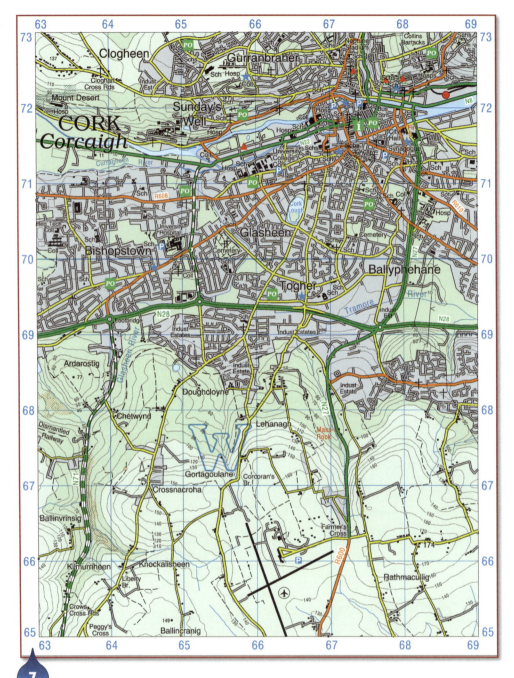

7

_____
_____
_____
_____
_____
_____
_____
_____

_____

_____

_____

_____

_____

_____

_____

14 '*Cork City is an important centre of tertiary economic activities.*'
Examine the above statement with reference to the map in Figure 7.

_____

_____

_____

_____

_____

_____

_____

_____

_____

_____

_____

_____

_____

Word puzzle

This puzzle is based on the Killarney area map on page 152 of your textbook.

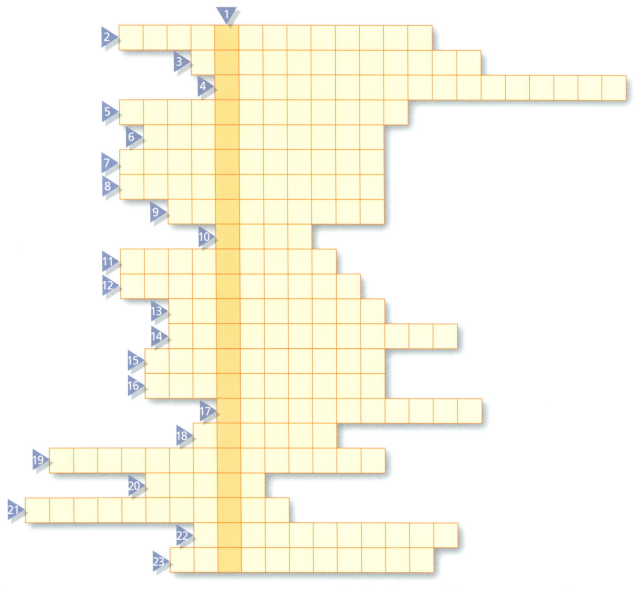

Down

1   A ratio (in this case 1:50,000) that is used to show scale

Across

2   Feature at V 984 886
3   Lakeside feature at V 912 892
4   Located at V 940 863
5   Second largest lake on map
6   Basic service at V 972 847
7   Island at V 93 89
8   Waymarked walk shown on south of map
9   Drainage pattern at V 98 83
10 Mountain at V 956 839
11 Largest settlement shown on map

12 Area in square kilometres represented on map
13 Area (in square kilometres) represented by map to the west of Easting 94 and to the south of Northing 90
14 On Muckross Lake
15 Recreational amenity at V 960 894
16 Recreational amenity at V 959 891
17 Not a smooth island south east of Innisfallen
18 Antiquity at V 971 882
19 Battle site at V 979 842
20 Direction of river flow at V 96 88
21 Sign of tourism at V 909 924
22 Place name suggests cirque at V 90 86
23 This map's statement of scale is two of these to one kilometre

14 Aerial Photographs

1 Types of aerial photograph

What types of aerial photographs are shown in Figure 1 below (part of Wicklow town), Figure 4 on page 83 (Carlow town) and Figure 6 on page 85 (Carrigaline)?

Indicate your answer by ticking the correct boxes below.

	Vertical	Low oblique	High oblique
Wicklow			
Carlow			
Carrigaline			

2 Locating features on aerial photographs

Indicate the location of each of the following features on the photographs listed below.

Use accepted notations, such as *right background*, etc. in the case of an oblique photograph; and *top left*, etc. in the case of a vertical photograph.

Figure 1:

● Sea cliffs _____

● A small roundabout _____

● The tip of a pier _____

● Depositions of silt or sand _____

● A ship _____

Figure 4 (Carlow town), page 83:

● A large blue-roofed building _____

● A church _____

● A weir _____

● A footbridge _____

● A large riverside park _____

1

3 Identifying features on aerial photographs

Link each of the features labelled **A** to **T** in Figures 2 and 3 with the correct feature in the list below. Indicate whether each is a physical or a cultural feature by ticking the appropriate box in each case.

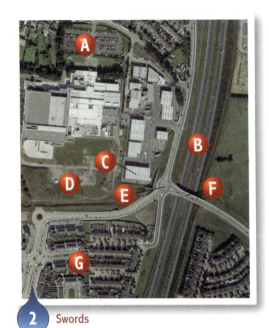

2 Swords

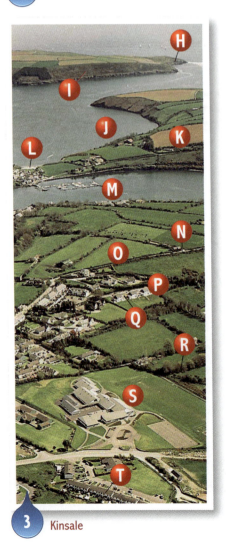

Label	Feature	Physical feature	Cultural feature
◯	Bay	◯	◯
◯	Bungalow	◯	◯
◯	Car park	◯	◯
◯	Country road	◯	◯
◯	Deciduous trees	◯	◯
◯	Field under pasture	◯	◯
◯	Field with ripe cereal crop	◯	◯
◯	Headland	◯	◯
◯	Housing estate	◯	◯
◯	Motorway	◯	◯
◯	Motorway flyover	◯	◯
◯	Roundabout	◯	◯
◯	Sandy beach	◯	◯
◯	School	◯	◯
◯	Sea cliff	◯	◯
◯	Semi-detached houses	◯	◯
◯	Small factory	◯	◯
◯	Terraced houses	◯	◯
◯	Undeveloped industrial site	◯	◯
◯	Yachting marina	◯	◯

3 Kinsale

4 Indicate the **season of the year** in which each photograph listed in the box was taken.
In each case, provide an explanation for your answer.

Hint: *in your explanations state the* location *of each* **feature** *you refer to.*

Photograph	Season	Explanation
Figure 3 (Kinsale), page 80		
Figure 4 (Carlow town), page 83		
Figure 6 (Carrigaline), page 85		

5 Calculate the **direction in which the camera was pointing** when each of the following photographs was taken:

- The photograph of Carlow town in Figure 4, page 83. (Also consult the OS map of Carlow on page 75.)

- The photograph of Carrigaline in Figure 6, page 85. (Consult the OS map and the photograph of Carrigaline on page 85 together.)

6 Sketch maps

In the space below, draw a sketch of the photograph of Carlow town in Figure 4 on the next page. Draw your sketch to half the scale (half the length and half the width) of the photograph. On your sketch, show and label an example or zone of each of the following land uses:

- industrial (manufacturing)
- commercial
- recreational
- religious.   (20 marks)

* Draw all four sides of the sketch accurately.

Frequently asked in Higher Level and Ordinary Level Leaving Certificate examinations

Higher Level marking scheme

- Outline of sketch: 4 marks (graded according to accuracy of scale and shape).
- Four land uses @ 4 marks each   = 16 marks
  Allocate each 4 marks as follows:
  - Naming land use: = 2 marks
  - Showing land use example/zone: = 2 marks, graded according to accuracy
- **Total**   = **20 marks**

4 Carlow town

7 More on sketch maps

(a) In the space below, draw a sketch to *half the scale* of the photograph of Carrigaline that appears in Figure 6.

(b) Show and name on your sketch each of the following *land use zones*:

- residential
- manufacturing and commercial
- religious.

(c) Show and name four different *traffic management devices* that are employed in the area shown on the photograph.

5 Carrigaline, Co. Cork

6 Carrigaline, Co. Cork

Ordinary Level question, marking scheme and sample answer

Question

8 Examine the **aerial photograph** of Carrigaline on page 85. Imagine that you have the task of finding a suitable location for a factory making computer software.

(a) State clearly where you would locate the factory using the usual notation (e.g. 'right background', etc.)

(b) Explain one reason in favour of this location and one reason against it.

(30 marks)

Ordinary Level marking scheme

- State suitable location using correct notation: = 6 marks
- Explain one reason in favour and one reason against the location: 12 + 12 marks = 24 marks

Allocate each 12 marks as follows:
- Reason stated: = 3 marks
- Reason explained:
  3 SRPs @ 3 marks each = 9 marks

Total = 30 marks

Sample answer

I would locate the factory in the large field in which silage is being cut on the <u>right background</u> of the photograph. ✔   6 marks

One <u>reason in favour</u> of this location is that the site itself is suitable for a factory. ✔   3 marks

The site is large enough to facilitate a large plant and an employees' car park with enough space left over for possible future expansion. ✔ The site is flat, which would reduce the difficulty (and therefore the cost) of constructing a factory on it. ✔ The site contains no existing buildings, the removal of which would increase the cost of building the factory. ✔   3 SRPS = 9 marks

A <u>reason against</u> the location is that it is adjacent to a large housing estate that is located on the right background of the photograph. ✔   3 marks

The entrance to the factory would have to be via the relatively narrow road adjoining the housing estate and this would increase traffic congestion in the vicinity of the housing estate. ✔ It might also create road hazards for children and other people living in the housing estate. ✔ Traffic to and from the factory (especially trucks or other heavy vehicles) might also create noise pollution in the vicinity of the housing estate. ✔   3 SRPS = 9 marks

30/30

9 Examine the aerial photograph of Carlow Town in Figure 4, page 83.

(a) Identify a suitable location for a large new post-primary school in the area shown in the photograph.

(b) Explain two reasons in favour of the location that you have chosen and one reason against that location.

10 '*OS maps and aerial photographs each have advantages in the way that they portray landscape.*'

Referring to the OS map and the aerial photograph of Carrigaline in Figure 6 on page 85, describe three advantages of OS maps and three advantages of aerial photographs as a means of portraying landscape. Refer in your answer to the location of features and/or other evidence on the OS map and photograph.

Advantages of OS maps

1 _____
_____
_____
_____
_____
_____

2 _____
_____
_____
_____
_____
_____

3 _____
_____
_____
_____
_____
_____

Advantages of aerial photographs

1 _____
_____
_____
_____
_____
_____

2 _____
_____
_____
_____
_____
_____

3 _____
_____
_____
_____
_____
_____

15 Skill Development – Statistics, Graphs, Charts and Images

1 Tables of statistics

The data in Figure 1 relate to new vehicles registered in Ireland over a period of six years. Examine Figure 1 and answer the questions that follow.

Vehicle	2001	2002	2003	2004	2005	2006
Private cars	160,908	150,485	142,992	149,635	166,270	173,273
Goods vehicles	30,622	28,412	30,532	31,165	38,396	43,619
Tractors	2,681	2,868	2,970	2,881	3,168	3,687
Motor cycles	6,919	5,596	4,993	3,833	3,240	3,206
Other new vehicles	2,602	2,268	2,600	2,894	3,359	3,773
Total	203,732	189,629	184,087	190,408	214,433	227,558

1 New vehicles registered in Ireland 2001–2006

Source: CSO

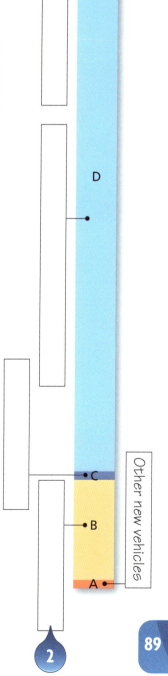

2

(a) How many private cars were registered in 2006? _____

(b) How many tractors were registered in 2004? _____

(c) What was the total number of vehicles registered in 2003? _____

(d) Which type of vehicle showed the smallest increase from 2004 to 2005? _____

(e) In which year was the fewest number of vehicles registered? _____

(f) In which year was the greatest increase in (total) vehicle registration recorded? _____

(g) In 2006, what *percentage* of total vehicle registration consisted of private cars? _____

(h) The percentage bar in Figure 2 refers to types of new vehicles registered in 2001. In the spaces provided, write the type of vehicle referred to by each of the labels **B** to **E**.

2   Examine the diagram in *Figure 3* and answer the questions that follow.

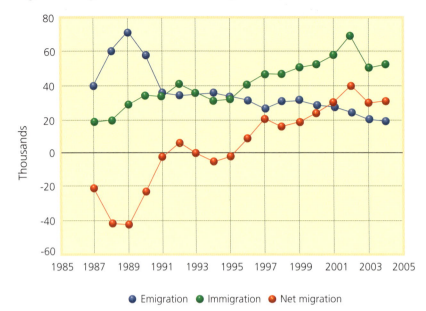

Title: _____

(a) Write a suitable title for Figure 3 in the space provided under the diagram.

 (b) In what year did the greatest number of people
    emigrate from Ireland?   _____

(c) How many people immigrated to Ireland in 1988?   _____

(d) List any two-year period in which emigration
    showed an increase.   _____

(e) In which year did the number of emigrants
    first equal the number of immigrants?   _____

(f) What do you think is meant by the term
    '*net migration*'?   _____

    _____

(g) In which year was net migration at its highest?   _____

(h) State one factor, other than those listed in
    the diagram, that would cause a change in the
    total population of Ireland.   _____

(i) Name another type of diagram that could be used
    to illustrate the information contained in Figure 3.   _____

3 Examine the chart in Figure 4 and answer the questions that follow.

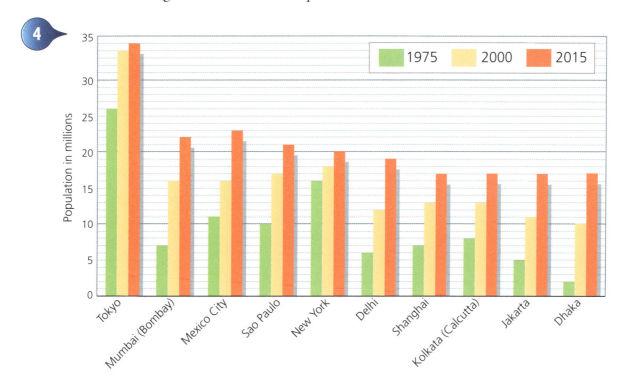

4

(a) What was the population of Tokyo in 2000? _____

(b) Which city had the smallest population in 1975 and
what was its population at that time? _____

(c) By how many millions is the population of Mexico City
expected to grow between 1975 and 2015? _____

(d) Which city is expected to have the lowest increase in
population between 2000 and 2015? _____

(e) Which city experienced the fastest rate of
increase in population between 1975 and 2000? _____

(f) Which city is expected to have the slowest rate of
increase in population between 1975 and 2015? _____

(g) Use Figure 4 to identify the cities that are represented as **A**, **B** and **C** in Figure 5.
Write the name of each city in the space provided in Figure 5.

	1975	2000	2015	Name of city
City A	10	17	21	
City B	8	13	17	
City C	11	16	23	

5 Population (in millions) of three cities in 1975, 2000 and 2015 (projected)

4 Drawing charts

The table in Figure 6 refers to the populations of four cities in 1956 and 2006.

	1956	2006
City A	129,991	149,256
City B	76,032	129,789
City C	115,501	133,839
City C	82,090	115,002

6

Use the space below to design and draw a graph/chart that shows the data given in Figure 6.

Hints

Make sure your graph/chart contains all of the following:

- A suitably labelled *vertical axis*.
- A suitably labelled *horizontal axis*.
- A suitable *title*.

5 Percentage (stacked) bars

The stacked bar charts in Figure 7 show percentage agricultural land uses in a Co. Kilkenny farm in 1982, 1991 and 2000.

(a) What percentage of the farm was under barley in 1991?

_____

(b) By what percentage did permanent pasture increase between 1982 and 1991?

_____

(c) Which crop occupied the same area in 1982 and 1991?

_____

(d) Which crop never occupied more that 7% of the farm from 1982 to 2000?

_____

(e) By what percentage did permanent pasture exceed wheat and barley combined in 2000?

_____

(f) Which land use showed the smallest percentage decrease between 1982 and 2010?

_____

(g) The percentage land use figures for the same farm in 2010 were as follows:
- Permanent pasture   51%
- Wheat   11%
- Barley   6%
- Silage   19%
- Others   13%

Complete the 2010 bar graph to show the above statistics. (You may *label* land uses instead of using colour coding.)

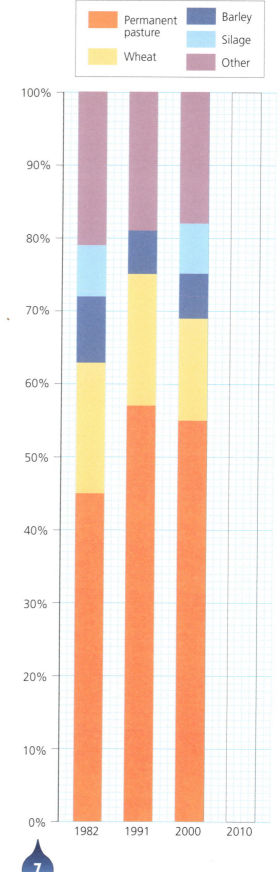

Country	A	B
Primary sector	18	4
Secondary sector	31	28
Tertiary sector	51	68

8

6 Drawing charts

The table in *Figure 8* shows the percentages of people employed in three economic sectors in two countries. Using the graph paper area on this page, draw a suitable graph/chart to illustrate this data.

7 Pie charts

Examine the pie chart in Figure 9 and answer the questions that follow.

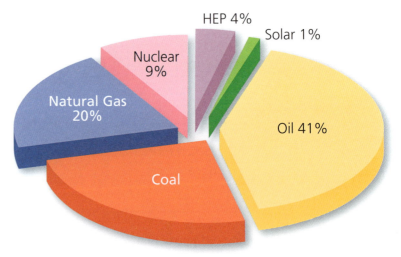

Energy Sources USA (2003)

9

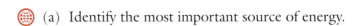 (a) Identify the most important source of energy.

_____

(b) Identify one type of fossil fuel listed in the chart.

_____

(c) What percentage of energy was produced from coal?

_____

(d) What percentage of energy was produced from renewable sources?

_____

(e) By what percentage did oil and natural gas combined exceed all other listed sources of energy?

_____

8 Choropleth map

The map in Figure 10 shows household disposable incomes (relative to the national average) in Ireland in 2002. Examine Figure 10 and answer the questions that follow.

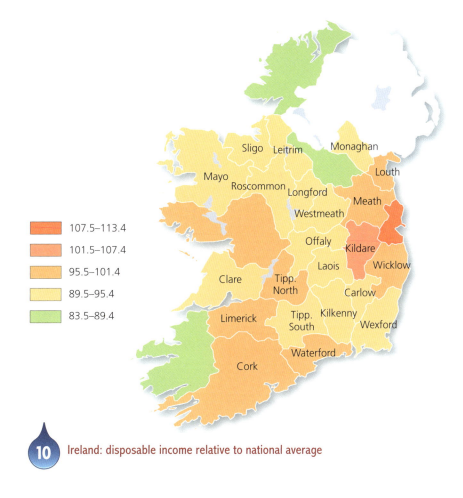

Legend:
- 107.5–113.4
- 101.5–107.4
- 95.5–101.4
- 89.5–95.4
- 83.5–89.4

10 Ireland: disposable income relative to national average

(a) Identify the county with the highest disposable income. _____

(b) Name the three counties with the lowest disposable income.

_____   _____   _____

(c) Give one reason why the counties referred to
    in (b) above had low disposable incomes. _____

_____

(d) What was the disposable income in Co. Galway relative to the national average?

_____

(e) Rank the following counties according to their disposable income:
    Cavan; Dublin; Kildare; Kilkenny; Limerick.

1 _____ (highest)   4 _____

2 _____   5 _____ (lowest)

3 _____

9 Triangular graph

The triangular graph in Figure 11 shows levels of clay, sand and silt in various classes of soil. Examine Figure 11 carefully before answering the questions that follow.

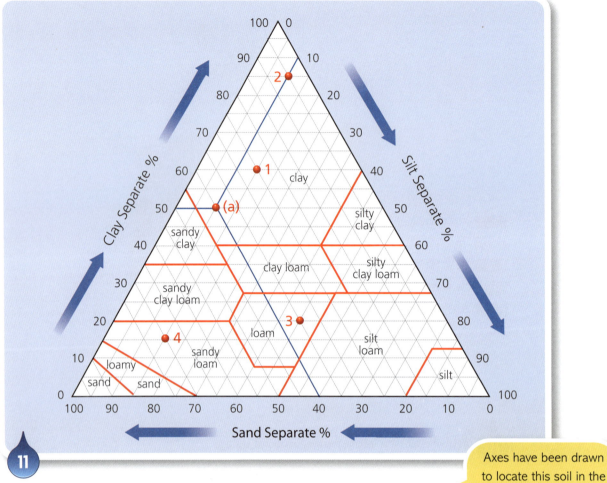

11

Classify the soils with the following compositions:

(a) 50% Clay + 40% Sand + 10% Silt _____clay_____

(b) 10% Clay + 30% Sand + 60% Silt _____

(c) 20% Clay + 45% Sand + 35% Silt _____

(d) 65% Sand + 30% Silt + 5% Clay _____

> Axes have been drawn to locate this soil in the graph. You should draw suitable axes to locate the positions of soils (b), (c) and (d).

Write the percentages of clay, silt and sand that make up each of the soils labelled **1** to **4** on the graph. To help you do this, draw radiating axes from the location of each label.

1 Clay _____% + Silt _____% + Sand _____%

2 Clay _____% + Silt _____% + Sand _____%

3 Clay _____% + Silt _____% + Sand _____%

4 Clay _____% + Silt _____% + Sand _____%

10 Population pyramids

Figure 12 shows three population pyramids labelled **A**, **B** and **C**. These pyramids show the population structures in Japan in 1950, 2010 and 2050 (projected). They also show the percentages of *young dependants* (aged 0–14), of *elderly dependants* (aged 65 and over) and of people in the 'economically active' age group of 15 to 64.

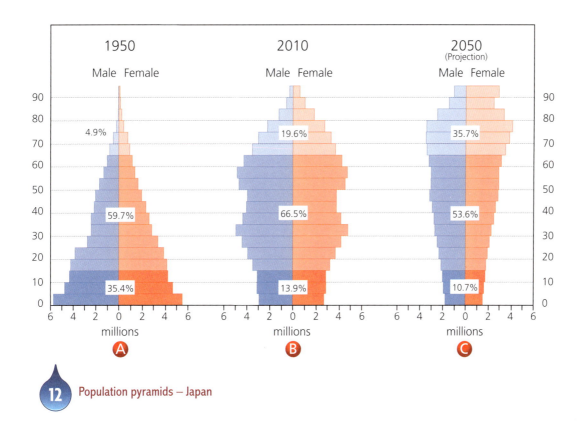

12 Population pyramids – Japan

(a) What percentage of the population was in the 15–64 age group in 1950? _____

(b) Which age group (0–14, 15–64 or 65 and over) will have shown the greatest increase between 1950 and 2050? _____

(c) What (total) percentage of the population was classified as dependent in 2010? _____

(d) Identify one socio-economic problem that might arise from the high percentage of the population aged 65 and over in 2050.

_____

_____

_____

11 Examine the data in Figure 13, which shows Ireland's population by age and sex in 2010. Using graph paper (provided below), draw a suitable graph to illustrate this data.

Age group	% Male	% Female
0–14	21%	20%
15–24	15%	15%
25–44	32%	31%
45–64	22%	22%
65 +	10%	12%
Total	100%	100%

Ireland's population by age and sex 2010 **13**

Marking scheme

- Title (must reflect the title of Figure 13): = 2 marks
- Appropriate use of graph paper: = 2 marks
- Scaled vertical axis: = 2 marks
- Five items illustrated correctly: 2 marks each (graded) = 10 marks
- Overall presentation: = 4 marks (graded)

Total **= 20 marks**

Hint

A population pyramid is the normal way of presenting this information. But bar graphs or pie charts (more difficult) were also accepted.

12 Weather chart

Examine the weather chart in Figure 14 and answer the questions that follow.

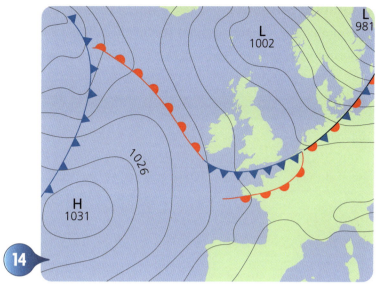

14

(a) Match each weather map symbol in Column A with its description in Column B.

Column A	
A	🔴🔴🔴
B	🔺🔺🔺🔺
C	
D	H 1022

Column B		
1	Warm front
2	Isobars
3	Anticyclone
4	Cold front

A	
B	
C	
D	

(b) Identify the type of front that is shown over northern Germany. _____

(c) State the barometric pressure at the centre of the depression shown to the north of Scotland. _____

(d) Calculate the barometric pressure at the western tip of Co. Kerry. _____

(e) Are winds stronger or weaker over Ireland than over southern Norway? How do you know?

_____

_____

(f) According to this chart, what weather conditions would you expect to find in northwest France?

_____

_____

13 Climate statistics

Examine the temperature and precipitation figures for Gibraltar and Moscow shown in Figure 15. Then answer the questions that follow.

	J	F	M	A	M	J	J	A	S	O	N	D
Gibraltar												
Temp. (°C)	12.8	13.3	14.0	16.0	18.3	21.0	22.7	24.0	21.6	19.0	15.5	13.3
Rainfall (mm)	129	107	122	69	43	13	0	2.5	34.5	84	167	138
Moscow												
Temp. (°C)	−11.0	−9.5	−4.5	3.0	11.7	16.7	19.0	17.2	11.0	4.5	2.0	−8.0
Rainfall (mm)	28.0	22.8	30.5	38.0	48.0	51.0	71.0	74.0	45.0	35.5	40.6	38.0

15

(a) State the mean temperature of the hottest month in Gibraltar. _____

(b) Which is the wettest month in Moscow? _____

(c) Calculate the annual temperature ranges in Gibraltar and Moscow.

 Gibraltar: _____ **Moscow:** _____

(d) Calculate the total annual precipitation in Moscow. _____

(e) Which of the two places – Gibraltar or Moscow – experiences a mild, wet winter and a hot, dry summer? _____

(f) Using the graph paper section on this page, draw suitable graphs to illustrate temperatures and precipitation levels in **Moscow** for the months of **March**, **April** and **May**. Give your chart a title.

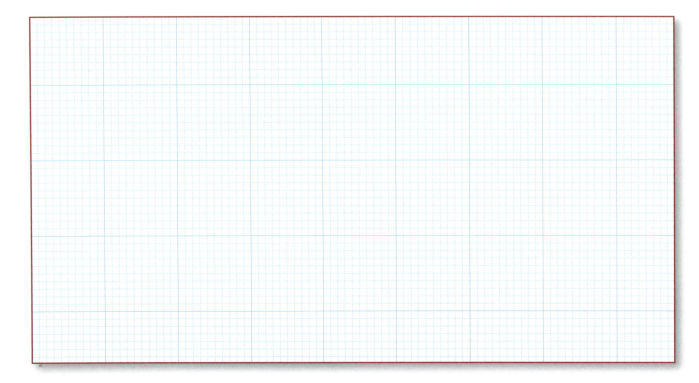

14 The **satellite map** in Figure 15 is a radar image of the Dublin area taken from a US space shuttle. Link each of the labels **A–L** on the map with its corresponding feature in the list given below.

highly populated area

mountainous area

15

(Bull) **sea wall and breakwater**	⬤	(Irish) **Sea**	⬤	(Dublin) **Mountains**	⬤
Densely populated (city**) area**	⬤	**Headland** (Dalkey)	⬤	(Dublin) **Airport**	⬤
(Dun Laoghaire) **Harbour**	⬤	(Sutton) **Tombolo**	⬤	**River** (Liffey)	⬤
Sand spit (Portmarnock)	⬤	(Ireland's Eye) **Island**	⬤	**Railway line**	⬤

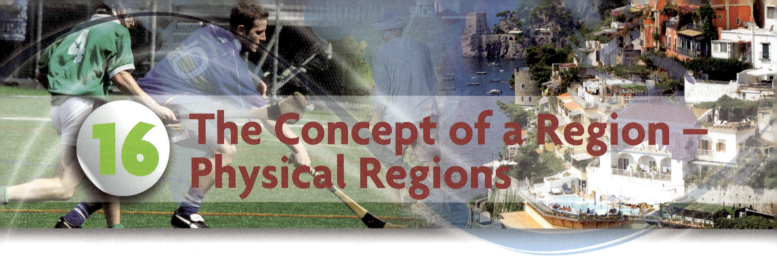

1 What is meant by the geographical term *region*?

_____

_____

_____

_____

2 List five **different types** of geographical region.

(a) _____

(b) _____

(c) _____

(d) _____

(e) _____

3 Name three examples of *climatic regions* and three examples of *geomorphological regions* that can be found in Europe.

Climatic regions	Geomorphological regions
(a) _____	(a) _____
(b) _____	(b) _____
(c) _____	(c) _____

4 Insert and label each of the following regions on the outline map of Europe in Figure 1.
- A region of cool temperate oceanic climate.
- A region of Mediterranean climate.
- The North European Plain (shade in pencil).
- A karst region.
- The south Munster ridge and valley region.

1 An outline map of Europe

5 Each photograph and quotation on this page relates to conditions in one of the regions that you were asked to insert on the outline map in Figure 1. Write the name of the appropriate region under each photograph or quote.

This region of parallel synclines and anticlines facilitates east–west movement across the countryside.

This region stretches across the western margins of Europe from northern Spain to northern Norway.

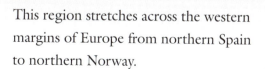

6 Examine the synoptic chart (weather map) of a winter's day in Ireland (Figure 2).

(a) In the spaces provided, write the letter used on the weather map to label each of the weather features listed below.

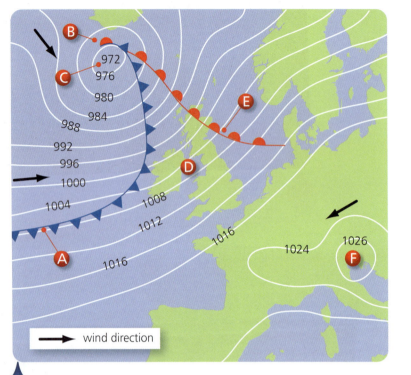

Weather feature	Letter
Warm front	◯
Cold front	◯
Occluded front	◯
Warm sector	◯
Centre of cyclone	◯
Centre of anticyclone	◯

2 Weather map of a winter's day in Ireland

(b) What is the barometric pressure:

• at the centre of the cyclone? _____

• at the centre of the anticyclone? _____

(c) Describe the likely weather conditions over Ireland that are indicated on the weather map. Refer briefly to each of the following.

• Atmospheric pressure: _____

• Wind speed (strong or weak): _____

• Wind direction: _____

• Cloud type and cover: _____

• Precipitation: _____

(d) Assuming that the cyclone shown on the map was moving eastwards, forecast the *changes in weather* that Ireland might have experienced when the front labelled **A** passed over the country.
Refer briefly to each of the following.

● Change in temperature _____

_____

● Change in cloud type and cover _____

_____

● Change in precipitation _____

_____

7 Consult the table of statistics in Figure 4 on page 199 of your textbook.
Using these statistics, draw suitable graphs on the squared area provided here to show the following.

● Mean temperatures for January, February and March.

● Amounts of rainfall for January, February and March.

● Give your graph a title.

Title: _____

_____

_____

16.0   17.0
15.0   16.0
14.0   15.0
13.0   14.0
12.0   13.0
     mm
11.0   12.0
10.0   11.0
9.0   10.0
8.0   9.0
7.0   8.0
6.0   7.0

January   February   March

8 A region is an area that has one or more characteristics that distinguish it from other areas. Describe the key characteristics of a geomorphological region of your choice.

_____

_____

_____

_____

_____

_____

_____

_____

_____

_____

_____

_____

_____

_____

_____

_____

_____

_____

_____

_____

_____

_____

_____

Higher Level Leaving Certificate marking scheme

- Name the region: = 4 marks
- Development/examination: 8 SRPs* @ 2 marks each = 16 marks

Total = 20 marks

* Try to **exceed the number of SRPs** required.

17 The Concept of a Region – Administrative and Cultural Regions

1 Identify an example of and give one descriptive statement about each type of region listed below. One example and description has been provided for you.

	Type of region	Example	Descriptive statement
1	A cultural (language) region in Ireland	Connemara Gaeltacht	A region where people's first language is Irish
2	A cultural (language) region in mainland Europe		
3	An administrative region in Ireland		
4	An administrative region in France		
5	A multinational cultural (religious) region		

2 Examine the map of Ireland in Figure 1.

(a) Name the regions or areas labelled **A**, **B** and **C** on the map.

A _____

B _____

C _____

(b) Name the type of local or regional body that would govern or manage each of the areas/regions labelled **A**, **C**, **D**, **E** and **F** on the map.

A _____

C _____

D _____

E _____

F _____

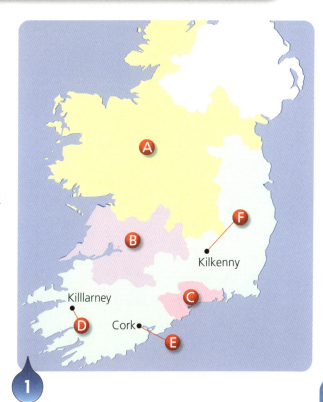

1

3 In the spaces provided below:

- List in rank order four types of administrative regions in the French Republic.
  (Begin with the largest type of region and end with the smallest type.)
- Make two descriptive statements about each type of region that you name.

	Type of region	Descriptive statements
1		(a) _____ _____ (b) _____ _____
2		(a) _____ _____ (b) _____ _____
3		(a) _____ _____ (b) _____ _____
4		(a) _____ _____ (b) _____ _____

4 Draw a map of Belgium in the box provided. On the map show and name each of the following:

- a French-speaking area
- a Dutch-speaking area
- a German-speaking area
- Brussels
- Antwerp
- part of the Netherlands
- part of France
- part of Germany.

5 *'Language has made Belgium a unique and problematic cultural region.'*
Examine the above statement fully.

_____

_____

_____

_____

_____

_____

_____

_____

_____

_____

_____

_____

_____

_____

_____

_____

_____

_____

_____

_____

_____

_____

_____

_____

_____

Marking scheme

- Two regions named @ 2 marks each   = 4 marks
- Development/examination:
  13 SRPs* @ 2 marks each**   = 26 marks
- **Total**   **= 30 marks**

* SRPs may include past or
present regional diversities or
problems and attempted
responses to problems.
** Try to **exceed the number of
SRPs** required.

6 (a) Identify the region shown on the
map in Figure 2.

_____

(b) Name three countries that are located
within the region shown.

1 _____

2 _____

3 _____

2

(c) Write a full account of the beliefs and customs that define the region shown.

_____

_____

_____

_____

_____

_____

_____

_____

_____

_____

_____

_____

_____

_____

_____

_____

_____

_____

_____

_____

Word puzzle

Down

1 BMW Region
2 Happened in 1609

To help your chapter revision.

Across

3 This type of council governs Drogheda
4 Type of administrative region in France
5 Bilingual capital of Belgium
6 French administrative region – larger than that in 4 across
7 *Dáil Éireann* sits in this House
8 Continent with many Islamic countries
9 One of eight Irish regions – includes Limerick
10 Irish city governed by a borough council
11 Works to create employment in Gaeltacht regions
12 Some unionists march on the twelfth of this month
13 Pilgrimage to Mecca
14 Tower attached to a mosque
15 This county contains a Gaeltacht region
16 Home of Walloons
17 Holiest city for Muslims
18 Another continent with many Islamic countries
19 'The _____' began in Northern Ireland in the late 1960

20 Islamic place of worship
21 Islam's word for God
22 Islam is the leading religion in this Asian country
23 There are 75 of these councils in Ireland
24 Leading nationalist political party in Northern Ireland
25 Home to Belgium's Flemings
26 Large port in area of 25 across
27 The religion practised by Muslims
28 Principal language of Wallonia
29 Principal language of Flanders
30 Islamic country in Middle East
31 Many Northern Ireland nationalists support this Glasgow football club
32 Some Ulster Unionists call themselves this
33 Forbidden to Muslims
34 Smallest type of French administrative unit

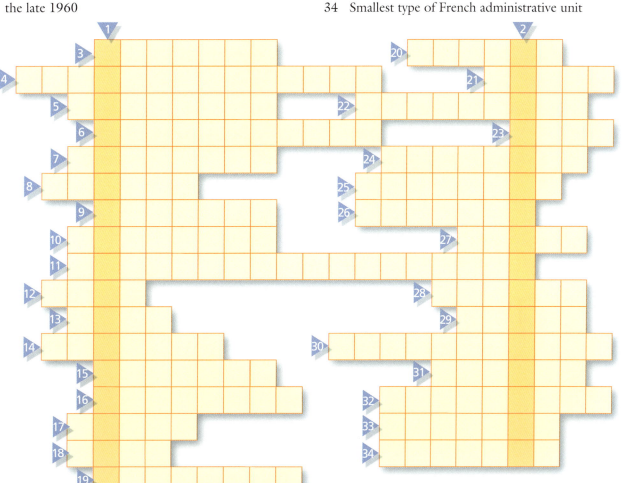

18 The Concept of a Region – Socio-economic and Urban Regions

1 Write two matching examples or descriptions for each of type of region listed below.
Select items from the Selection Box for your examples.

Type of region	Example	Description
Climate region		
Geomorphological region		
Administrative region		
Cultural region		
Socio-economic region		
Urban region		

Selection Box
departments   Munster Ridge and Valley region   conurbation   Arctic
region of industrial decline   North European Plain   Connemara Gaeltacht
Irish counties   core region   cool temperate oceanic   Islamic world

2 Link the **region type** (letter) with an **example in Europe** (number) in the box provided.
One has been completed for you.

Region Type		Example in Europe		Letter	Number
A	Industrial	1	Alps	A	6
B	Mountain	2	North Italian Plain/Paris Basin	B	
C	Climatic	3	Mezzogiorno	C	
D	Core	4	Mediterranean	D	
E	Cultural	5	Irish Gaeltacht	E	
F	Less developed	6	Nord/Pay de Calais	F	

3

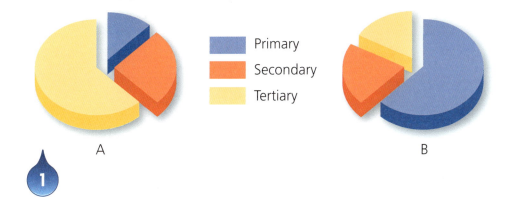

A   B

1

Examine the pie charts, which represent a core region and a peripheral region, in Figure 1. Answer the following questions.

(a) Identify which chart, **A** or **B**, represents a core region. _____

(b) State one example of a peripheral region in Europe.

_____

(c) Define one characteristic that defines a core region. _____

_____

(d) Define one characteristic that defines a peripheral region. _____

_____

4 On the map in Figure 2 show and name each of the following:
  ● Europe's central core region
  ● two secondary core regions
  ● two peripheral regions.

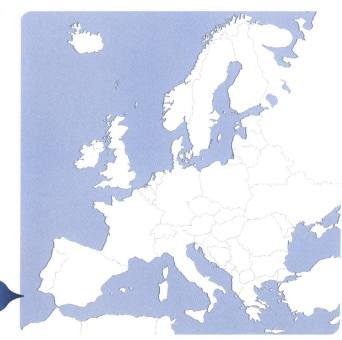

2

5 Match each of the region types in **Column A** with its description in **Column B**.

Column A		Column B	
A	Geomorphological regions	1	Local councils, corporations, constituency boundaries, county divisions, etc
B	Cultural regions	2	Less-developed regions, core regions, peripheral regions, regions of industrial decline
C	Administrative regions	3	Regions based on distinctive landforms, e.g. karst landscapes, ridge and valley landscapes, plains, etc.
D	Socio-economic regions	4	Regions associated with language and religion

A	
B	
C	
D	

6 With the aid of a sketch map, write an account of a named *European region of industrial decline*.

Sketch map

_____
_____
_____
_____
_____
_____
_____
_____
_____
_____
_____
_____
_____
_____
_____
_____
_____
_____
_____
_____
_____
_____
_____
_____
_____
_____
_____
_____

Marking scheme

- Name region: = 2 marks
- Development/examination:
  11 SRPs* @ 2 marks each = 22 marks
- Labelled sketch map = 6 marks

Total = **30 marks**

On your sketch map, show and name the region you are writing about, the country in which the region is located and four relevant places and/or features in the region.

* Try to **exceed the number of SRPs** required.

🌐 **7** Match each of the region types in **Column X** with the correct example in **Column Y**.

Column Y	
A	Climatic region
B	Administrative regions
C	Socio-economic regions
D	Cultural region
E	Urban region
F	Physical region
G	Peripheral region

Column X	
1	Paris
2	Ireland's counties
3	Mezzogiorno
4	Cool temperate oceanic
5	Basque
6	Core and peripheral
7	The Alps

A	
B	
C	
D	
E	
F	
G	

8 Explain each of the following terms briefly but clearly.

● **Urban zone of influence** _____

_____

_____

● **Nodal point** _____

_____

_____

● **Commuter belt** _____

_____

_____

● **Urban sprawl** _____

_____

_____

● **Primate city** _____

_____

_____

● **Conurbation** _____

_____

_____

9

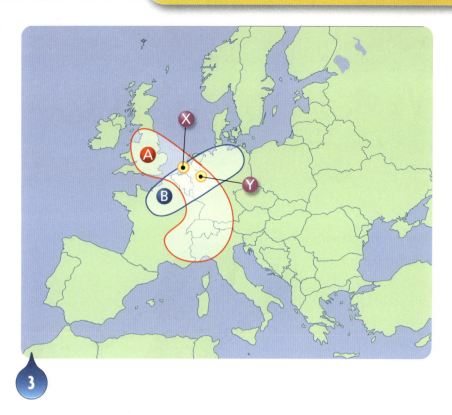

3

(a) Name and make two statements about each of the urban axes labelled **A** and **B** on the map in Figure 2 above.

Urban axis **A**:

● *Name:* _____

● *Statement (i)* _____

● *Statement (ii)* _____

Urban axis **B**:

● *Name:* _____

● *Statement (i)* _____

● *Statement (ii)* _____

(b) What is meant by the term *conurbation*? _____

_____

(c) Name the conurbations labelled **X** and **Y** on the map in Figure 3.

X _____ **Y** _____

19 The West – An Irish Region

1 In the box below, draw a sketch map of Ireland. Show and name **one** Irish **region**. In that region, show and name the following:

- one mountain area
- one river
- one urban centre
- one major routeway.

Frequently asked question

2 Physical processes in the West

Complete the passage below by **circling** the correct alternatives and **inserting** the missing words.

Like all of Ireland, the West has a cool _____ oceanic-type climate. But the West tends to experience *more/less* precipitation than most other Irish regions. This is because _____ rainfall is common in mountainous areas and because of the frequency of frontal or _____ rainfall. The prevailing south-_____ winds and the warm North _____ Drift help keep winters mild and temperature ranges moderate. Figure 1 shows the following information about climatic conditions at Belmullet in Co. *Mayo/Galway*.

- The average temperature for the warmest month is _____°C and for the coldest month _____°C, giving an annual temperature range of _____°C.

- The total annual rainfall is *more/less* than 1,100mm. Rainfall shows a *summer/winter* maximum.

Although soils vary throughout the West, they are generally of *excellent/poor* quality. Much of the West's mountains are covered in *peaty/brown* soils that are frequently waterlogged and poorly drained. Other poorly drained soils include P_____ and G____. Brown soils are common in the *western/eastern* parts of the region and are generally the *most/least* fertile in the West.

Mountains in the West were folded during C_____ times and include ranges such as the Twelve ____. Glaciation during the P_____ Ice Age led to the formation of *erosional/depositional* features such as cirques in the mountains. The *erosional/depositional* features shown in the photograph are _____. A rise in sea level following the Ice Age led to the formation of a ___ or drowned river valley at Killala Bay and a drowned glacial valley called a _____ at Killary Harbour.

Drainage features include the river Suck, which is a tributary of the river _____, and lakes such as Lough _____, which is the largest lake in the Republic of Ireland. Drumlin swarms *impede/stimulate* drainage. This sometimes gives rise to *dendritic/deranged* drainage patterns and to *poor/good* drainage.

Month	J	F	M	A	M	J	J	A	S	O	N	D
Temp (°C)	5.5	6.1	7.1	8.5	10.6	12.6	14.0	13.5	13.0	10.7	8.1	6.8
Rainfall (mm)	133	95	100	64	65	67	72	98	101	139	132	133

1 Average monthly temperatures and rainfall at Belmullet in 2000

Higher Level question, marking scheme and sample answer

 3 Examine two factors that have influenced the development of primary activities in any Irish region that you have studied. **(30 marks)**

Marking scheme

- Name region = 2 marks
- Identify two primary activities: 2 + 2 marks = 4 marks
- Name two factors: 2 + 2 marks = 4 marks
- Examination: 10 SRPs @ 2 marks each = 20 marks

Hints:

- *Link your discussion to the region named. Otherwise score no more than 4 SRPs in 'examination' section.*
- *Discuss two factors. Otherwise score no more than 4 SRPs in 'examination' section.*

The region that I will discuss is the <u>West</u>, which comprises Counties Mayo, Galway and Roscommon.

Region: 2 marks

<u>Farming</u> in the West concentrates mainly on the rearing of sheep and dry cattle, rather than on better-paying cattle fattening or tillage. ✔

Activity: 2 marks

Factor: 2 marks

One factor that causes this is the generally <u>infertile soils</u> that are common in the region.

In parts of west Co. Galway, the underlying rock is granite, which breaks down into poor clay soils when weathered. ✔ Rain-drenched mountains such as the Twelve Pins are covered mainly in peaty soils. ✔ These soils are infertile because they are shallow and have poor mineral content. ✔ Heavy rainfall leads to severe leaching in places such as east Mayo. ✔ Severe leaching makes soil infertile because it washes plant nutrients down through the soil and out of reach of plant roots. ✔ Some good-quality brown earth soils are present in east Galway. ✔ But even those are too shallow to suit tillage farming and so they are used instead for cattle rearing. ✔

<u>Fishing</u> in the West has been favoured by the favourable <u>condition of the Atlantic Ocean</u> off the west coast.

Activity: 2 marks
Factor: 2 marks

The North Atlantic Drift keeps fishing ports such as Rossaveal ice-free throughout the year. ✔ It also helps to mix nutrients in the seas off the west coast, thus encouraging the growth of a variety of fish species such as mackerel, herring and cod. ✔ Sunlight can penetrate the shallow continental shelf that lies off Ireland. ✔ This encourages the growth of microscopic plankton on which many fish species feed. ✔ Seas off the West of Ireland are relatively clean and free of biotoxins and other pollutants. ✔ This is important for the welfare of all fish life, but especially for shellfish such as oysters and mussels that are farmed in Galway Bay and Killary Harbour. ✔

30 / 30

4 Describe and explain any two physical factors that have influenced the development of agriculture in an Irish region that you have studied. (30 marks)

_____

_____

_____

_____

_____

_____

_____

_____

_____

_____

_____

_____

_____

_____

_____

_____

_____

_____

_____

_____

_____

Marking scheme

- Name region: = 2 marks
- Name two physical factors: 2 + 2 = 4 marks
- Examination: 12 SRPs* @ 2 marks each = 24 marks

Total = **30 marks**

Hints:
- Discuss two physical factors
- Link your discussion to the region named by giving regional examples, etc.

* Try to **exceed the number of SRPs** required.

5 Examine the development of secondary economic activities in an Irish region
   that you have studied.   (30 marks)

_____

_____

_____

_____

_____

_____

_____

_____

_____

_____

_____

_____

_____

_____

_____

_____

_____

Marking scheme

- Name region: = 2 marks
- Name two secondary activities: 2 + 2   = 4 marks
- Examination: 12 SRPs* @ 2 marks each   = 24 marks

Hints:
- Write about **one Irish** region.
- **Link** your examination to the **region** you name.
  Otherwise score no more than 6 SRPs.

* Try to **exceed the
number of SRPs** required.

6 Use the boxes to match each item in **Column X** with its appropriate description in **Column Y**.

Column X	
A	Údarás na Gaeltachta
B	Regional Development Fund
C	Industrial Development Agency
D	European Social Fund
E	Common Fisheries Policy
F	Common Agricultural Policy

Column Y	
1	Introduced quotas to stem the depletion of stocks
2	Implemented an interventionist policy to prevent big falls in the prices of products
3	Is especially focused on developing Irish-speaking areas
4	Sets up ready-to-occupy factories to attract overseas manufacturing companies
5	Supports the retraining of unemployed workers
6	Provides grants for industrial training and for the upgrading of roads and other transport networks

A	
B	
C	
D	
E	
F	

7 Examine the bar graphs in Figure 2. Indicate whether each of the following statements is true or false by circling the correct option.

(a) There were more than 400,000 people in Mayo in 1841.

True / False

(b) The population of Galway has always been greater than that of Mayo.

True / False

(c) Roscommon has the smallest population of the three counties shown.

True / False

(d) Population trends in Galway differ from those in Roscommon and Mayo.

True / False

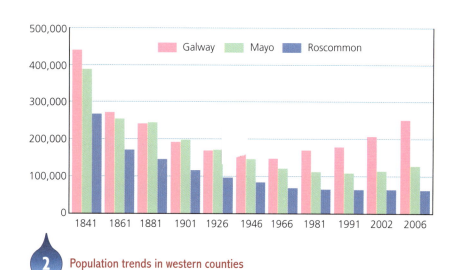

2 Population trends in western counties

🌐 8 Tourism – interpreting statistics

The statistics below refer to the number of visitors to Ireland and the reasons why they come to Ireland.

Number of Visitors to Ireland (Thousand)						
	1999	2000	2001	2002	2003	2004
Business	994	1,074	975	906	854	926
Holiday/leisure/recreation	3,306	3,346	3,177	3,242	3,334	3,413
Visits to friends/relatives	1,439	1,564	1,566	1,603	1,736	1,807
Other	328	328	273	314	445	429
Total	6,067	6,312	5,991	6,065	6,369	6,575

3   Details of numbers of visitors to Ireland 1999–2004 and reason for journey   (Source: Central Statistics Office)

(a) In which year did the largest number of tourists come to Ireland? _____

(b) How may visitors came to Ireland in 2001? _____

(c) Write down the reason most visitors give for coming to Ireland.

_____

(d) How many visitors gave 'visits to friends/relatives' as a reason in 2001? _____

(e) In which year did the fewest number of tourists come to Ireland? _____

9 Tourism to the West – interpreting map data

Examine the map data on tourism to the West of Ireland that is given in Figure 4.
Then answer the following questions.

(a) State the percentage of tourists who originated from each of the following places:

- Ireland (domestic) _____

- Britain _____

- North America _____

(b) Name **one place** where each of the following tourist attractions can be found. Use map evidence *only*.

(i) A long-distance path

_____

(ii) A sandy beach (give approximate location)

_____

(iii) A national park

_____

(iv) A great house or castle open to the public

_____

(v) A house and gardens open to the public

_____

(vi) A cathedral or abbey

_____

(vii) A tourist centre

_____

(c) Describe one problem that mass tourism can bring to a region.

_____

_____

_____

_____

_____

_____

_____

_____

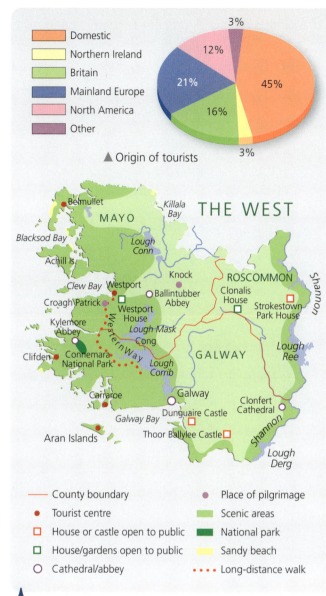

Origin of tourists

Domestic
Northern Ireland
Britain
Mainland Europe
North America
Other

3%
12%
21%
45%
16%
3%

THE WEST

Belmullet
MAYO
Killala Bay
Blacksod Bay
Lough Conn
Achill Is
Knock
ROSCOMMON
Shannon
Clew Bay Westport
Croagh Patrick
Ballintubber Abbey
Clonalis House
Strokestown Park House
Westport House
Kylemore Abbey
Lough Mask
Cong
Western Way
Clifden
Connemara National Park
Lough Corrib
GALWAY
Lough Ree
Carraroe
Galway
Dunguaire Castle
Clonfert Cathedral
Galway Bay
Thoor Ballylee Castle
Shannon
Aran Islands
Lough Derg

County boundary
Tourist centre
House or castle open to public
House/gardens open to public
Cathedral/abbey
Place of pilgrimage
Scenic areas
National park
Sandy beach
•••• Long-distance walk

4 Data on tourism in the West of Ireland

10 Examine the development of tertiary economic activities in an Irish region that you have studied. (30 marks)

_____

_____

_____

_____

_____

_____

_____

_____

_____

_____

_____

_____

_____

_____

_____

_____

_____

_____

_____

_____

_____

_____

_____

_____

Higher Level marking scheme

- Name region: = 2 marks
- Name two tertiary activities: 2 + 2   = 4 marks
- Examination: 12 SRPs* @ 2 marks each   = 24 marks

  Total   = 30 marks

Hints:
- Write on **one** Irish region.
  In your examination **refer to the region** you name.
  Otherwise score no mark for 'examination'.

* Try to **exceed the number of SRPs** required.

11 Describe the influence of the European Union on any named Irish region that you have studied. (30 marks)

_____

_____

_____

_____

_____

_____

_____

_____

_____

_____

_____

_____

_____

_____

_____

_____

_____

_____

_____

_____

_____

_____

_____

Ordinary Level marking scheme

- Name region: = 3 marks
- Describe the importance of the EU.
  Use 9 SRPs* @ 3 marks each = 27 marks

Total = 30 marks

Suggested Higher Level marking scheme

- Name region = 2 marks
- Describe the importance of the EU.
  Use 14 SRPs* @ 2 marks each = 28 marks

Total = 30 marks

* Try to **exceed the number of SRPs** required.

20 The Greater Dublin Area – an Irish Region

1 (a) In the box provided, draw a sketch map of Ireland.

On your map, show and name **two** contrasting regions.

(b) For each region, show and name:

- one relief feature
- one drainage feature
- one urban centre.

2 The tables of statistics in Figure 1 show mean monthly temperatures and monthly precipitation at Belmullet, Co. Mayo and at Dublin Airport in a single year.

Belmullet, Co. Mayo	Jan	Feb	Mar	Apr	May	Jun	Jul	Aug	Sep	Oct	Nov	Dec
Mean temperature (°C)	5.5	5.9	6.8	8.3	10.3	12.6	13.9	14.0	12.6	10.8	7.7	6.6
Precipitation (mm)	123	80	96	58	68	67	68	93	108	134	128	120

Dublin Airport	Jan	Feb	Mar	Apr	May	Jun	Jul	Aug	Sep	Oct	Nov	Dec
Mean temperature (°C)	5.1	5.6	6.2	7.7	10.1	13.0	14.8	14.6	12.7	10.3	7.2	6.0
Precipitation (mm)	70	51	54	51	55	56	50	71	67	68	65	76

1

(a) Use the statistics to fill in the information in the grid below.

		Belmullet	Dublin Airport
A	Name of the warmest month		
B	Mean temperature of the coolest month		
C	Amount of precipitation during the driest month		
D	Annual temperature range		
E	Total annual precipitation		

(b) Use the squared paper to illustrate graphically the **monthly precipitation levels** at **Dublin Airport**. (Label the vertical and horizontal axes appropriately. Give your work a title.)

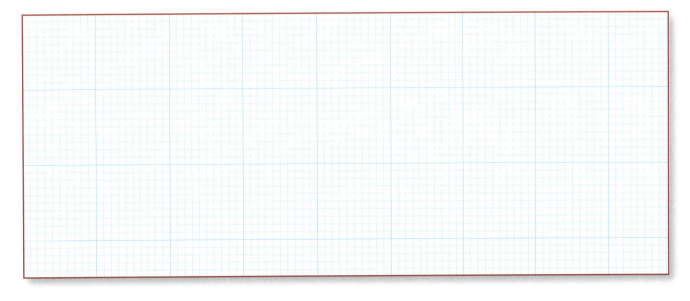

3 Examine the development of secondary activities in an Irish region that you have studied. (30 marks)

_____

_____

_____

_____

_____

_____

_____

_____

_____

_____

_____

_____

_____

_____

_____

_____

_____

_____

_____

_____

_____

_____

_____

_____

_____

Higher Level marking scheme

- Name the Irish region: = 2 marks
- Name two secondary activities: 2 + 2 = 4 marks
- Examination: 12 SRPs @ 2 marks each = 24 marks

Total = **30 marks**

Hints

- If your answer does not refer to a particular Irish region you will score no marks for your 'examination'.
- Up to two examples can count as SRPs.
- Try to exceed the number of SRPs required.

4 The graph in Figure 2 shows the percentage of people employed in a selection of economic activities in the Greater Dublin Area (GDA) and in an area of the Western region of Ireland.

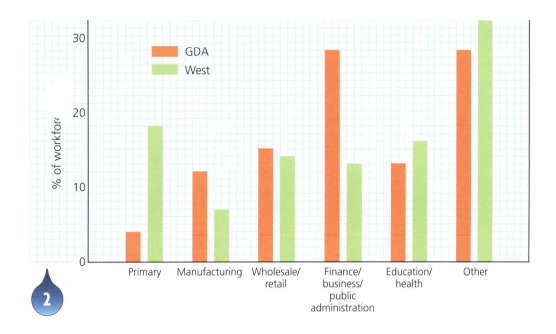

2

(a) For each area, rank the three most important economic activities (or grouped activities) in terms of employment. Begin each ranking with the activity that gives most employment. Do not include the 'other' category in your rankings.

	GDA	**The West**
1	● _____	● _____
2	● _____	● _____
3	● _____	● _____

(b) Use the partly completed divided bars provided in Figure 3 to illustrate the information given in Figure 2

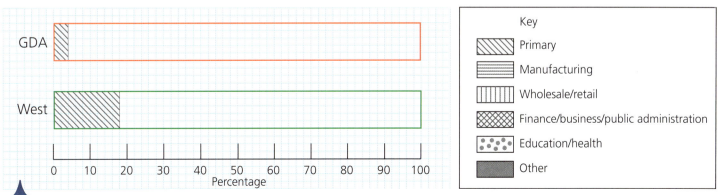

3

5 Examine the development of tertiary economic activities in an Irish region that you have studied. (30 marks)

_____
_____
_____
_____
_____
_____
_____
_____
_____
_____
_____
_____
_____
_____
_____
_____
_____
_____
_____
_____
_____
_____
_____
_____
_____
_____

Marking scheme

- Name the Irish region: = 2 marks
- Name two tertiary activities: 2 + 2 = 4 marks
- Examination: 12 SRPs @ 2 marks each = 24 marks

Total = **30 marks**

Hints
- If your answer does not refer to a particular Irish region you will score no mark in your 'examination'.
- Try to exceed the number of SRPs required.

6 Population structures in areas of Dublin

The population pyramids labelled **1**, **2** and **3** represent population structures in the areas of Dublin labelled **A**, **B** and **C** on the map in Figure 4.

Indicate which area is represented by each population pyramid and explain the reasons for your choice.

● **Pyramid 1** represents area: _____

  My reasons: _____

  _____

  _____

● **Pyramid 2** represents area: _____

  My reasons: _____

  _____

  _____

● **Pyramid 3** represents area: _____

  My reasons: _____

  _____

  _____

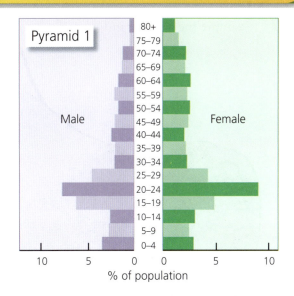

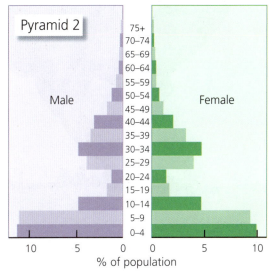

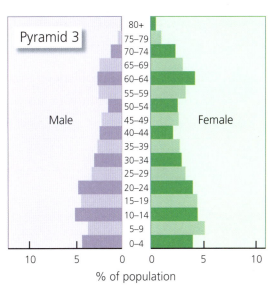

7 Examine the cartoon in Figure 5.

5

BRICKS

(a) What urban problem does this cartoon refer to and what point is it making?

_____

_____

_____

_____

_____

_____

_____

_____

_____

_____

_____

_____

_____

_____

(b) Describe how the problem referred to in the cartoon might be reduced or controlled. Refer in your answer to the Greater Dublin Area.

_____

_____

_____

_____

_____

_____

_____

8 Contrasting regions

Contrast two Irish regions that you have studied under the headings of *physical processes* and *economic processes*.

I will contrast the <u>West</u>✓ and the <u>Greater Dublin Area</u> (GDA).✓

Physical Processes

Precipitation in the West (1,100mm annually at Belmullet) is much heavier than in the GDA (750mm annually in Dublin).✓ This is because the West receives much relief and cyclonic rain from the Atlantic, while the GDA is in the rain shadow of the western mountains.✓ _____

_____

_____

_____

_____

_____

_____

_____

_____

Economic Processes _____

_____

_____

_____

_____

_____

_____

_____

_____

_____

_____

21 The Paris Basin – a European Region

1 Examine the maps of the Paris Basin and Paris in Figure 1. Match each of the places labelled **A–P** on the map with the corresponding place on the grid provided. One match has been made for you.

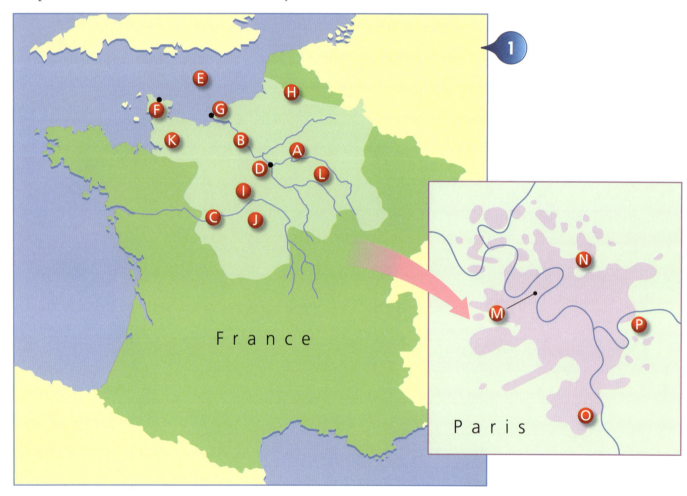

1

France

Paris

H	Artois
	Beauce
	Cherbourg
	Dry Champagne
	Evry
	La Defense

	English Channel
	Le Havre
	River Loire
	River Marne
	Marne-la-Vallée

	Normandy
	Paris
	River Seine
	Sologne
	St Denis

2 Examine the development of primary activities in one non-Irish European region of your choice. (20 marks)

_____
_____
_____
_____
_____
_____
_____
_____
_____
_____
_____
_____
_____
_____
_____
_____
_____
_____
_____
_____
_____
_____
_____
_____
_____

Marking scheme

- Region named: = 2 marks
- Two primary activities named: 2 + 2 = 4 marks
- Examination: 7 SRPs @ 2marks each = 14 marks

Total **= 20 marks**

Hints

- Only a non-Irish European region will be accepted.
- Try to exceed the number of SRPs required.

3 The grid below shows the names of four areas in the Paris Basin. In the spaces provided, write a soil type, an agricultural activity and an associated secondary activity that matches each area. Choose the appropriate entries from the Selection Box.

Place	Soil type	Agricultural activity	Associated secondary activity
Île de France			
Brie			
Dry Champagne			
Sologne			

Selection Box
dairy farming   sandy soil   wine making   loess   chalk-based soils   forestry
viticulture   flour milling   cheese making   clay   wheat growing   saw milling

4 In the box provided, draw a map of the Paris Basin. In your map show and name each of the following:

- the River Seine
- the River Loire
- Côte d'Or
- Paris
- Orléans
- Île de France
- Brie
- Dry Champagne
- Sologne.

5 Select a non-Irish European region and explain how (a) relief and (b) climate have influenced the development of its agriculture. (30 marks)

Leaving Certificate Higher Level Sample Paper

_____

_____

_____

_____

_____

_____

_____

_____

_____

_____

_____

_____

_____

_____

_____

_____

_____

_____

_____

_____

_____

_____

* Try to **exceed the number of SRPs** required.

Suggested marking scheme

- Region named: = 2 marks
- Discussion of relief:
  7 SRPs* @ 2 marks each = 14 marks
- Discussion of climate:
  7 SRPs* @ 2 marks each = 14 marks

Total = **30 marks**

6 Explain the importance of **one** of the primary industries listed below to the economy of any European region studied by you:

- agriculture
- forestry
- fishing
- mining/energy.   (30 marks)

_____

_____

_____

_____

_____

_____

_____

_____

_____

_____

_____

_____

_____

_____

_____

_____

_____

_____

_____

_____

_____

_____

Ordinary Level marking scheme

- Naming the region: = 6 marks
- Explaining the importance of the primary industry chosen to the economy of the region: = 24 marks
  8 SRPs* @ 3 marks each

  Total   = **30 marks**

* Try to **exceed** the number of **SRPs** required.

7 Examine the development of manufacturing industry in a European region – not Ireland – of your choice. (30 marks)

_____

_____

_____

_____

_____

_____

_____

_____

_____

_____

_____

_____

_____

_____

_____

_____

_____

_____

_____

_____

* Try to **exceed the number of SRPs** required.

Hints

- You **must** write on a non-Irish European region.
- If you do not link your answer to the region you name, you cannot score more than 8 SRPs for your discussion.
- Up to three examples can count as SRPs.

Higher Level marking scheme

- Name region: = 2 marks
- Discussion:
  14 SRPs* @ 2 marks each = 28 marks
  Total = **30 marks**

8 Name one European region – not Ireland – that you have studied.
Describe the development of the tourist industry in that region.   (40 marks)

_____

_____

_____

_____

_____

_____

_____

_____

_____

_____

_____

_____

_____

_____

_____

_____

_____

_____

_____

_____

_____

Ordinary Level marking scheme

● Name region: = 4 marks
● Development/examination:
   12 SRPs* @ 3 marks each   = 36 marks

Total   = 40 marks

* Try to **exceed** the number of SRPs required.

Hints
● You must name a non-Irish European region.
● Relate your development to the region that you name.
● Examples can count for up to 3 SRPs.

9 Figure 2 shows the number of tourists who visited part of an *arrondissement* (district) in Paris and the number of local people who left that area to holiday elsewhere. Tourist movements were recorded on a monthly basis and are expressed in thousands of people.
Examine Figure 2 and answer the questions that follow.

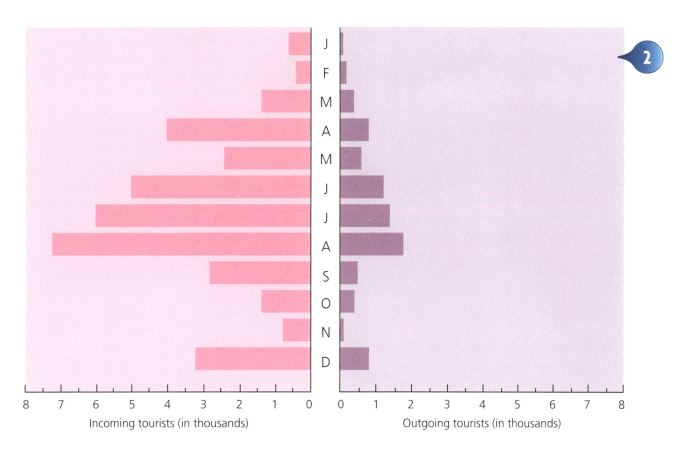

Incoming tourists (in thousands)   Outgoing tourists (in thousands)

(a) In which month was incoming tourism at its lowest? _____

(b) In which month was outgoing tourism at its highest? _____

(c) How many tourists came to the area in June? _____

(d) How many outgoing tourists left the area in September? _____

(e) Which month showed the highest *total* tourist movement and what was the

total tourist movement during that month?

Month: _____   *Total movement:* _____

(f) Indicate whether each of the following statements is *true* or *false*.

- The area shown is more a source than a destination area for tourists.   *True / False*

- There were more incoming tourists in March than there were
outgoing tourists in July.   *True / False*

- More than 30,000 tourists visited the area in the course of the year shown.   *True / False*

10 The chart in Figure 3 shows the number of tourists arriving in European countries in 2006. Examine the chart and answer the questions that follow it.

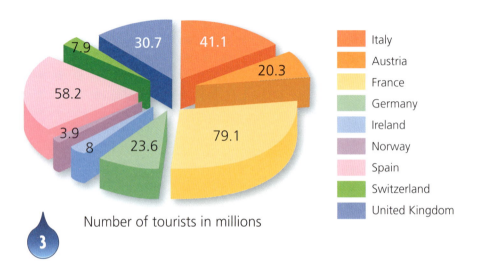

Italy
Austria
France
Germany
Ireland
Norway
Spain
Switzerland
United Kingdom

Number of tourists in millions

3

(a) Which country received the fewest number of tourists in 2006? _____

(b) Which country received the largest number of tourists in 2006? _____

(c) Calculate the difference between the highest and the lowest numbers of tourists arriving. _____

(d) How many tourists arrived in Germany in 2006? _____

(e) Which country received 7.9 million tourists in 2006? _____

(f) Calculate the total number of tourists that arrived in 2006 in the nine European countries referred to. _____

(g) Rank the nine countries referred to according to the number of tourists who arrived in them. Begin your list with the country that received the greatest number of tourists.

(i) _____   (ii) _____   (iii) _____

(iv) _____   (v) _____   (vi) _____

(vii) _____   (viii) _____   (ix) _____

11 The table of statistics in Figure 4 shows annual population change in an *arrondissement* (district) in Paris between 1960 and 2010. Examine the table and answer the questions that follow.

	1960	1970	1980	1990	2000	2010
Natural change	+550	+671	+728	+670	+498	+487
Migration to/from other parts of France	+410	+?	−220	−603	−641	−653
Migration to/from countries outside France	+ 453	+560	+410	+220	+360	+180
Total population change	+1,413	+1311	+918	+287	+217	+?

4

(a) Two figures have been omitted from the table and replaced by question marks. Calculate each of those figures and write it into the table.

(b) The following statements relate to the table of statistics. Indicate whether each statement is *true* or *false* (circle the correct alternative in each case).

- Natural change contributed more than migration to population growth in the arrondissement in 1960.   *True / False*

- From the 1980s onwards, there was net out-migration from this arrondissement to other parts of France.   *True / False*

- The total population of the arrondissement has declined gradually over time.   *True / False*

(c) What is meant by the term 'natural change', as used in the table? _____

_____

(d) Below is a partial description of *natural change* based on the table of statistics in Figure 4. Complete the description by circling the correct alternatives and by filling in the blank spaces in the description.

Natural change in the arrondissement in question has been constantly *positive / negative* in each of the years referred in the table. The natural increase in 1960 was _____. This increase became progressively larger up to the year _____, when the natural increase stood at _____.

From _____ to 2010, the rate of natural increase became gradually smaller. In _____ it stood at 670, and in 2000 it was _____. By 2010 the natural increase was _____.

The figures show that, in each of the years given, birth rates *were lower than / exceeded* death rates in the arrondissement in question.

Revision word puzzle

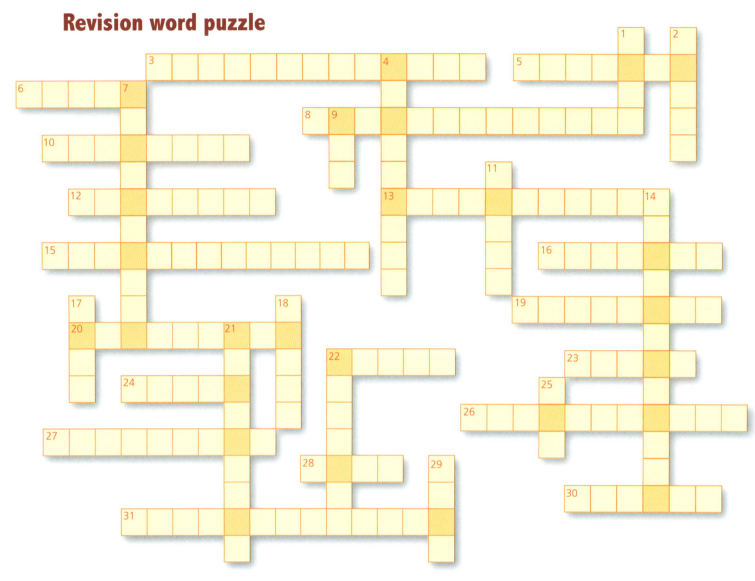

Across

3 Tourist town south of Paris with old royal palace and forest
5 North African former French colony
6 River on which Paris is located
8 Sports tourists flock to this stadium in Paris
10 Large downfold, as in the Paris Basin
12 Famous university in Paris
13 This Paris landmark attracts millions of tourists each year
15 Famous street in Paris
16 Sandy, forested area to the south of the Paris Basin
19 Contains historic beaches in the north of the Paris Basin
20 Famous cathedral in Paris
22 River on the south of the Paris Basin
23 Mainly underground rail system in Paris
24 Important crop in Île de France
26 The cultivation of vines
27 Large fishing port
28 New town in Paris
30 Famous perfume/fashion company
31 The climate in the Paris Basin is _____ oceanic

Down

1 French cheese and dairy farming area
2 Tributary of the River Seine
4 Planned 'node' area in Paris
7 Cuesta
9 *Trains de grande vitesse*
11 This Saint is another planned 'node' in Paris
14 Upgrading of decayed city areas
17 French national rail system
18 This town has a Gothic cathedral and is the centre of the Champagne wine industry
21 French motorway
22 Important commercial port
25 Gentle slope of escarpment
29 Medieval walled city

22 The Mezzogiorno – a European Region

 1 In the box below draw an outline map of the Mezzogiorno.

Show and name the following on your map:

- one mountain range
- two individual mountains
- three rivers
- four large urban centres
- five sea areas

2 Interpreting data

The synoptic chart in Figure 1 shows contrasting weather conditions over the Paris Basin and the Mezzogiorno. Use the boxes below to name the weather systems present and to describe briefly the likely weather conditions at Paris and at Naples.

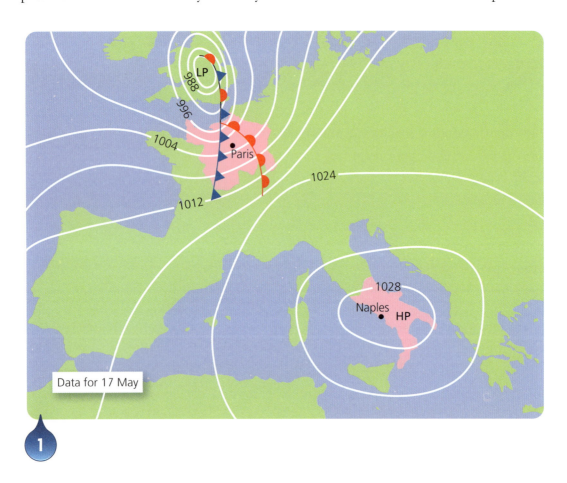

Data for 17 May

1

	Paris	Naples
Weather system		
Atmospheric pressure		
Temperature		
Cloud cover and type		
Precipitation		

3 Examine the photograph of Mount Vesuvius.

(a) On the photograph, label the **cone** and the **crater** of this volcanic mountain.

(b) Name one volcanic mountain, other than Mount Vesuvius, located in the Mezzogiorno.

_____

(c) State two advantages and one disadvantage of living in a volcanic region.

Advantages:

● _____

● _____

Disadvantage:

● _____

4 Interpreting data

The triangular graph in Figure 2 illustrates the percentages of workers engaged in primary, secondary and tertiary economic activities in three different *comuni* (local administrative areas) in Italy. The comuni are labelled **A–C** on the graph.

(a) In the table provided, write the percentages of workers engaged in primary, secondary and tertiary activities in comuni **A**, **B** and **C**.

(b) The table gives the employment structure of a fourth comune that is to be labelled **D**. Mark and label **D** in the correct position on the triangular graph.

Comuni	A	B	C	D
Primary activities				15
Secondary activities				20
Tertiary activities				65

Percentages of workers engaged in primary, secondary and tertiary activities in three Italian comuni

5 Examine the factors that influence the development of one economic activity*
in a European region (not Ireland) that you have studied.   (30 marks)

> * Write on **agriculture** in this instance.

Higher Level marking scheme

- Name economic activity: = 2 marks
- Name two factors: 2 + 2   = 4 marks
- Name region: = 2 marks
- Examination/development:
  11 SRPs @ 2 marks each   = 22 marks

Total   **= 30 marks**

Hints

- The region you name **must** be a non-Irish European region.
- If you do not refer to an appropriate region you will score nothing for the examination/development part of your answer.
- A mere description (without using examples, etc. from your chosen appropriate region) can score a maximum of only 5 SRPs (10 marks) in the examination/development part of the answer.
- A maximum of 2 SRPs (4 marks) can be given for examples.

_____

_____

_____

_____

_____

_____

_____

_____

_____

_____

_____

_____

_____

_____

_____

_____

_____

_____

_____

_____

_____

_____

_____

_____

_____

_____

Know your geographical terms

6 The terms listed below are all used in Chapter 22 of your textbook.
In the spaces provided, define each term briefly but clearly.

- *Mezzogiorno:* _____

  _____

- *Gross national product:* _____

  _____

- *Sirocco:* _____

  _____

- *Azores high:* _____

  _____

- *Terra rossa:* _____

  _____

- *Irrigation:* _____

  _____

- *Latifundia:* _____

  _____

- *Braccianti:* _____

  _____

- *Capital-intensive industries:* _____

  _____

7 Examine the development of industry or tourism in a European region – not Ireland – of your choice. (30 marks)

_____

_____

_____

_____

_____

_____

_____

_____

_____

_____

_____

_____

_____

_____

_____

_____

_____

_____

_____

_____

_____

_____

_____

_____

_____

_____

Higher level marking scheme

- Name region: = 2 marks
- Examination/discussion:
  14 SRPs @ 2 marks each = 28 marks

Total = **30 marks**

Hints

- Only a non-Irish European region will be accepted.
- The discussion must be linked to the specific region named, otherwise it can score only a maximum of 8 SRPs (16 marks).
- A maximum of three examples can count as SRPs.
- Try to exceed the number of SRPs required.

8 Examine Figure 3, which shows the average population densities of the eight sub-regions of the Mezzogiorno.

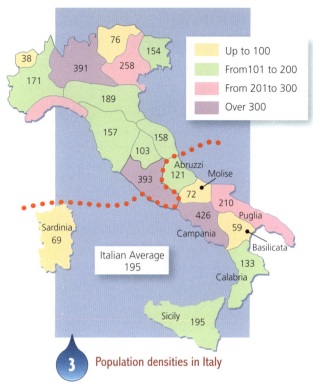

(a) In the spaces provided below, list the sub-regions of the Mezzogiorno that contain the following number of people per square kilometre:

- 426 _____

- 210 _____

- 195 _____

- 133 _____

3 Population densities in Italy

(b) Name two sub-regions in the Mezzogiorno that have higher population densities than the Italian average.

(i) _____   (ii) _____

(c) In the squared box provided, draw three bar graphs to show the population densities of **Basilicata**, **Molise** and **Sardinia**. Draw a vertical axis with a labelled scale and a horizontal axis that includes the names of the sub-regions. Give your work a suitable title.

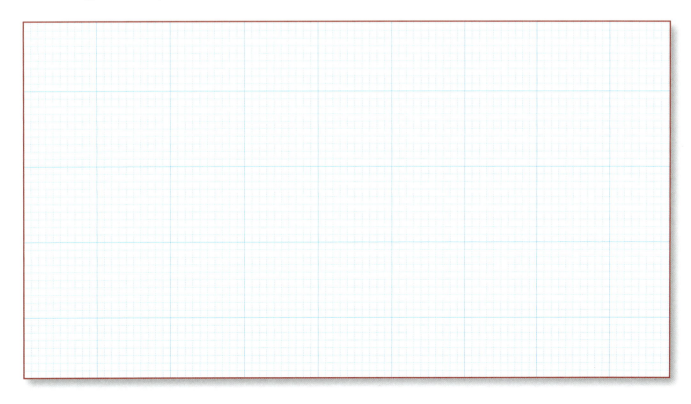

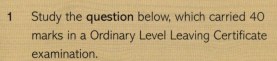

Exam training
Answering a forty-mark Ordinary Level question

1   Study the **question** below, which carried 40 marks in a Ordinary Level Leaving Certificate examination.
2   Study the official **marking scheme** for the question, which is also given below.
3   Then examine the **sample answer** given, which was allocated full marks in the examination.

> You can use the experience to help you answer other 40-mark Ordinary Level questions.

The question

Name one European region – not Ireland – that you have studied. Describe the development of **either** agriculture or the tourist industry in that region.   (40 marks)

The official marking scheme

- Name a European region (not Ireland):   = 1 mark
- Describe the development of the agriculture/tourist industry: = 39 marks
  13 SRPs @ 3 marks each

  Total   = **40 marks**

A sample full-mark answer

Region named = 1 mark

I will describe the development of agriculture in the <u>Mezzogiorno</u> region of Italy.

Each ✔ represents an SRP.

Several problems hindered the development of agriculture in the Mezzogiorno.

- The Mediterranean-type climate gives rise to prolonged dry periods in summer.✔ Summer drought traditionally limited the range of crops that could be grown,✔ so the cultivation of olives, vines, winter wheat and citrus fruits dominated farming.✔

- Steep and rugged relief hindered agriculture in the Apennines and other upland areas.✔ This relief made mechanised farming almost impossible and favoured poorly paying farming activities such as sheep rearing and the cultivation of tree crops.✔

- Most land in the Mezzogiorno was in the hands of rich landlords who owned large estates called latifundia.✔ Landlords rented tiny farms called minifundia to local peasants.✔ The peasant farmers had to give up to half of their produce to the landlords in rent.✔ They could not, therefore, make enough profit to improve their holdings or farming methods.✔

In 1950, the Italian government set up Enti di Riforma (Reform Agencies) and the Cassa per il Mezzogiorno ('Fund for the South') to reform agriculture and the economy of the Mezzogiorno.✔

The Enti di Riforma bought some latifundia and redistributed them among 100,000 landless peasant families.✔

The Cassa per il Mezzogiorno organised the digging of wells and the construction of reservoirs and irrigation schemes.✔ It trained peasant farmers to use their newly irrigated land to grow high-paying produce such as salad crops.✔ It built roads such as the Autostrada del Sole that helped to deliver farm produce to distant markets.✔ The Cassa built dwelling houses and outhouses on newly created farms.✔ It even organised the development of new villages that provided local farming communities with schools, clinics, shops and other services.✔

The achievements of the Enti di Riforma and the Cassa were incomplete. For example, only ten per cent of the Mezzogiorno was transferred from landlords to peasants.✔ Nevertheless, the reforms they carried out helped greatly to make farming more intensive and efficient throughout much of southern Italy.✔

40/40

9 With reference to two contrasting European regions (not Ireland),
explain the differences between them under **one** of the following headings:
climate; population patterns; energy sources; manufacturing industry. (40 marks)

_____

_____

_____

_____

_____

_____

_____

_____

_____

_____

_____

_____

_____

_____

_____

_____

_____

_____

_____

_____

_____

_____

_____

Ordinary Level marking scheme

- Name Region 1: = 5 marks
- Name Region 2: = 5 marks
- Explanations:
  10 SRPs* at 3 marks each
  (five SRPs must refer to Region 1
  and five SRPs to Region 2) = 30 marks

Total = **40 marks**

* Try to **exceed the number of SRPs** required.

10 Examine how the distribution of population, in a European region (not Ireland) that you have studied, has been influenced by the region's level of economic development.   (30 marks)

_____

_____

_____

_____

_____

_____

_____

_____

_____

_____

_____

_____

_____

_____

_____

_____

_____

_____

_____

_____

_____

_____

* Try to **exceed the number of SRPs** required.

Higher Level marking scheme

- Name the region: = 2 marks
- Refer to the distribution of population: = 2 marks
- Refer to associated economic development: = 2 marks
- Discussion: 12 SRPs* @ 2 marks each   = 24 marks

Total   **= 30 marks**

11 Contrasting geographical regions – interpreting data

Figure 4 on the facing page shows various comparisons between the North of Italy and the South of Italy.

(a) Use the information in Figure 4 to fill in the blanks and circle the correct **alternatives** in this passage:

In terms of **area**, the South of Italy is slightly *smaller / larger* than the North of Italy.

In terms of **population**, the South contains about _____ million people, while the

North contains *more / fewer* than 25 million. The population density of the North is about

_____ people per square kilometre, which is a *higher / lower* density than that of the

South. The birth rate and death rate bars show that there is a slight natural *increase / decrease* in the

population of the North and a slight natural *increase / decrease* in the South.

The **Gross Domestic Product** (GDP) of the North is almost _____ hundred billion

euro. This is about *three times / twice* the GDP of the South.

Employment by sector is shown by means of two *histograms / pie charts*. They reveal that _____%

of workers in the North and _____% of workers in the South are employed in agriculture.

(b) Does Figure 4 indicate that the North or the South of Italy is the more economically developed? Indicate your choice by ticking one of the boxes below.

The North ◯   The South ◯

(c) To what extent does the information given on *hospital beds, infant mortality rate* and *unemployment rate* support your answer to question (b) above? (Refer in your answer to figures given in Figure 4.)

● Hospital beds: _____

_____

● Infant mortality rate: _____

_____

● Unemployment rate: _____

_____

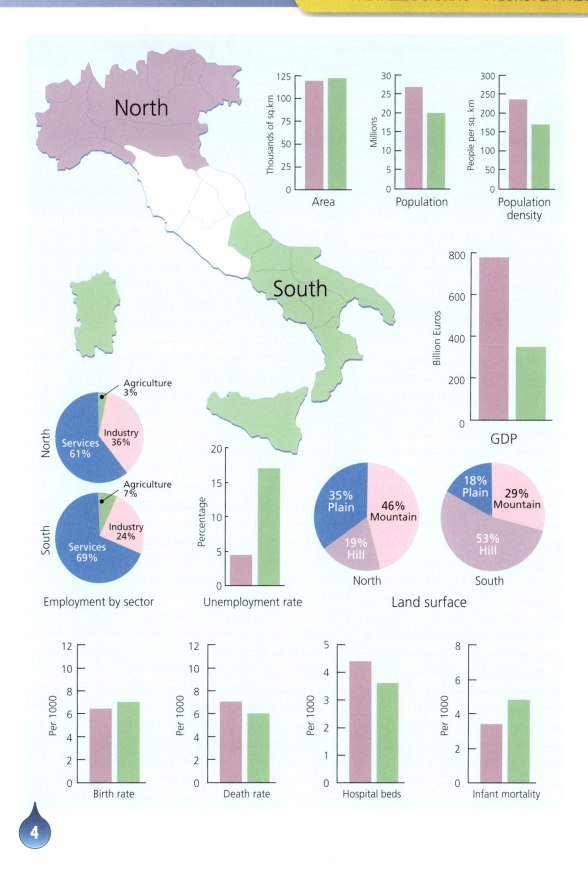

Area

Population

Population density

GDP

North

Agriculture 3%

Industry 36%

Services 61%

South

Agriculture 7%

Industry 24%

Services 69%

Employment by sector

Unemployment rate

North

35% Plain

46% Mountain

19% Hill

South

18% Plain

29% Mountain

53% Hill

Land surface

Birth rate

Death rate

Hospital beds

Infant mortality

4

23 India – a Sub-continental Region

1 Draw an outline map of a continental or sub-continental region. (Use the box provided.) On your map show and name the following:
- two physical landscape features
- two urban centres.

2 Show and name the following **additional** features on the outline map in the box above:
- one mountain range
- two rivers
- two cities
- two neighbouring countries
- two sea areas.

3 Link each of the photographs **A–F** with the appropriate title from the list below. Write the correct letters in the boxes provided.

Photograph titles   **Matching letters**

- The CBD of an Indian city

- A tea plantation in north-east India

- Modern manufacturing in India

- Part of a bustee in Mumbai

- A padi-field in the Ganges Plain

- Traditional manufacturing in India

4 In the case of a non-European continental or sub-continental region that you have studied, briefly describe **two** factors that have influenced the development of **agriculture** in the region.   (30 marks)

_____

_____

_____

_____

_____

_____

_____

_____

_____

_____

_____

_____

_____

_____

_____

_____

_____

_____

_____

_____

_____

_____

5 The table of statistics in Figure 1 refers to population by age in an area in southern India. Use the data in the table to complete the statements (a) – (f) and to carry out instruction (g) below.

Age group	Males	%	Females	%	Persons
0–14	1,731,665	14.3	1,690,057	14.0	3,421,722
15–24	1,822,390	15.1	1,721,190	14.2	3,543,580
25–44	1,352,878	11.2	1,342,297	11.1	2,695,175
45–64	872,110	7.2	900,145	7.5	1,772,255
65+	256,711	2.2	389,715	3.2	646,426
Total	6,035,754	50.0	6,043,404	50.0	12,079,158

1

(a) There were 1,342,297 females in the _____ age group.

(b) In the 15–24 age group there were _____ persons.

(c) The percentage of males in the 0–14 age group was _____% higher than the percentage of females.

(d) The number of females in the 65+ age group exceeded the number of males by _____.

(e) The total number of males was _____ fewer than the total number of females.

(f) The total number of persons was _____.

(g) Use the information in Figure 1 to complete the population pyramid in Figure 2 below.

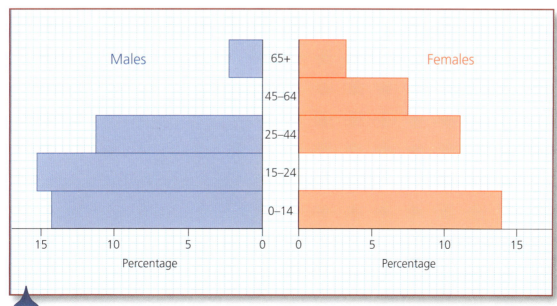

2

6 Examine the importance of **manufacturing industry** to any one non-European continental/sub-continental region that you have studied.
Clearly state the name of the region in your answer. (40 marks)

_____
_____
_____
_____
_____
_____
_____
_____
_____
_____
_____
_____
_____
_____
_____
_____
_____
_____
_____
_____
_____
_____
_____
_____

Official Ordinary Level marking scheme

- Name one region: = 1 mark
- Examine/describe the importance of industry in that region: = 39 marks
  13 SRPs* @ 3 marks each

Total = 40 marks

* Try to **exceed the number of SRPs** required.

7 Interpreting data

The statistics in Figure 3 show the principal religious affiliations of people in **India**, **Pakistan**, **Bangladesh** and **Sri Lanka**. The four pie charts labelled **A–D** also illustrate the principal religious affiliations in each of these countries, though the countries are not given in the same order as listed above.

(a) In the spaces provided, identify which country is illustrated by each pie chart.

	India	Pakistan	Bangladesh	Sri Lanka
Hindu	80		17	6
Muslim	17	97	81	8
Buddhist				69
Christian	1			6
Other	2	3	2	11

3 Religious affiliations (to nearest whole percentage point) in four Southern Asian countries

Pie chart	Country
A	_____
B	_____
C	_____
D	_____

(b) Use the information in Figure 3 to briefly **contrast** religious affiliations in India with religious affiliations in Sri Lanka.

_____

_____

_____

_____

_____

_____

_____

_____

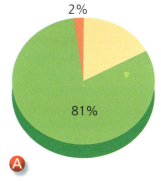

A — 2% / 81%

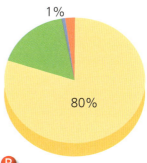

B — 1% / 80%

C

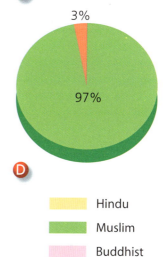

D — 3% / 97%

- Hindu
- Muslim
- Buddhist
- Christian
- Other

8 Describe the influence that **either** climate **or** physical landscape has on the development of **tourism** in any non-European continental or sub-continental region that you have studied. (30 marks)

_____

_____

_____

_____

_____

_____

_____

_____

_____

_____

_____

_____

_____

_____

_____

_____

_____

_____

_____

_____

_____

_____

_____

Official Ordinary Level marking scheme

- Name region: = 3 marks
- Describe the importance of tourism: = 27 marks
  9 SRPs* @ 3 marks each

  Total = **30 marks**

* Try to **exceed the number of SRPs** required.

9 Population densities in India

In the boxes provided, **identify** and **explain** the levels of population density in each of the four circled areas of India shown in Figure 4.

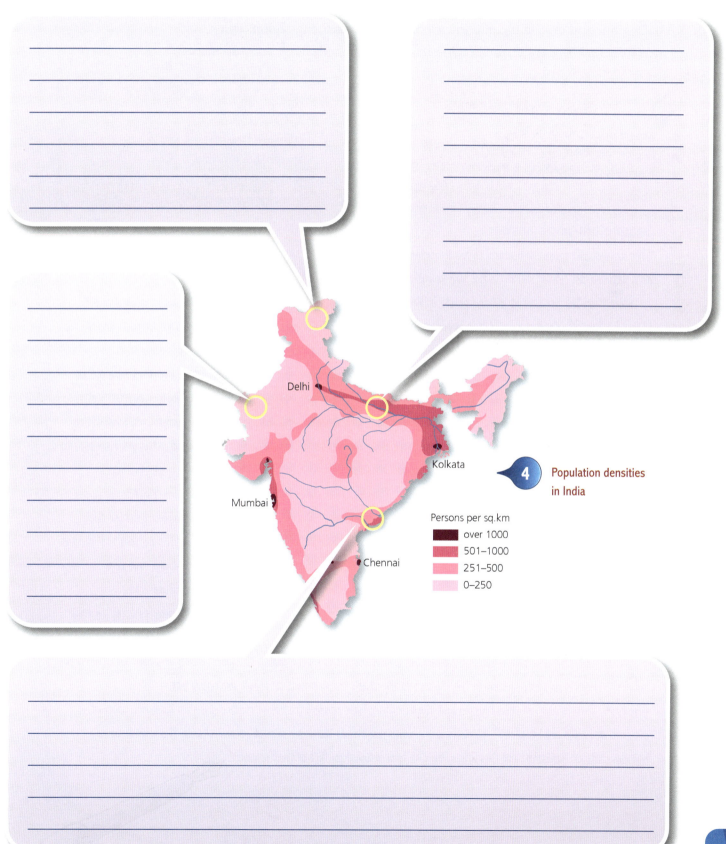

Delhi

Kolkata

Mumbai

Chennai

4 Population densities in India

Persons per sq.km
- over 1000
- 501–1000
- 251–500
- 0–250

Exam training
Higher Level thirty-mark question, marking scheme and sample answer

The question

10 Describe and explain the importance of culture in defining regions in a continental/sub-continental region that you have studied.   (30 marks)

Official marking scheme

- Aspect of culture identified: = 2 marks
- Region identified: = 2 marks
- Examination: 13 SRPs @ 2 marks each = 26 marks

Total   = **30 marks**

Hint
A discussion without reference to an appropriate region would get no mark.

Each ✔ represents an SRP.

Sample full-mark answer

This answer will focus particularly to the importance of religion *— Aspect of culture: 2 marks* as a defining aspects of culture in the sub-continent of India. *— Region named: 2 marks*

More than 80 per cent of Indians practise the Hindu religion and this affects the culture of India in many ways. ✔ Many Hindus are vegetarians and this is one reason why Indian agriculture is devoted more to growing crops than rearing animals. ✔

Hindus also believe that cows are sacred animals that may be milked and used to draw carts, but that may not be killed. ✔ This belief has resulted in a gradual growth in the numbers of cows in India to 200 million or one-fifth of the word's total. ✔ Old 'retired' cows are often allowed to roam unhindered through the streets of Indian towns, where they sometimes eat vegetables from street stalls and frequently contribute to traffic chaos. ✔ Some old cattle are even sent to special 'retirement homes' that are paid for by devout Hindus. ✔

The caste system is another offshoot of Hindu culture. ✔ This system divided Indian society into rigid social classes, each of which was defined by the work done by its class members. ✔ The highest class, for example, contained the Brahmins (priests) who had great influence over the social and political life of the country. ✔ At the bottom of the class system were the unfortunate Dalits or 'untouchables', ✔ who carried out work such as street cleaning and were considered to be 'unclean'. ✔ Hindus believed that, with patience and acceptance, one might in a future life be reincarnated into a higher caste. ✔ This helps to account for the passivity with which many untouchables accepted their inferior status in society. ✔

Other important religions in India include Islam, which has 200 million Indian followers, many of whom live in northern India. ✔ There is no caste system in the Muslim faith, which teaches that all people are equal before Allah (God). ✔ Differences between Muslim and Hindu culture have caused friction in regions such as Kashmir, where the majority of people are Muslim. ✔ Some local Muslims think that Kashmir should be united with the neighbouring Muslim state of Pakistan, and this has given rise to occasional conflict in that region. ✔

30/30

11 '*Culture is an important factor in defining some regions.*'
Examine the above statement with reference to any region
that you have studied.   (30 marks)

_____

_____

_____

_____

_____

_____

_____

_____

_____

_____

_____

_____

_____

_____

_____

_____

_____

_____

_____

_____

_____

_____

_____

Higher Level marking scheme

- Aspect of culture named: = 2 marks
- Region named: = 2 marks
- Examination: 13 SRPs @ 2 marks each   = 26 marks

Total   **= 30 marks**

Hints

- A second (but not a third) aspect of culture may be credited in the answer.
- The answer must relate to one named region.
- Try to exceed the number of SRPs required.

12 *'The boundaries of city regions have expanded over time.'*
Discuss this statement with reference to one example that
you have studied. (30 marks)

_____

_____

_____

_____

_____

_____

_____

_____

_____

_____

_____

_____

_____

_____

_____

_____

_____

_____

_____

_____

Higher Level marking scheme

- Name region: = 2 marks
- Reference to time or period in history: = 2 marks
- Discussion: 13 SRPs* @ 2 marks each = 26 marks

Total = **30 marks**

* Try to **exceed the number of SRPs** required.

Hints
- Discussion can refer to describe/explain/discuss.
- Refer to the expansion of one city only.

13 Word puzzle – India

Across

1 Desert region in north-west India
2 This 'Revolution' affected agriculture
3 Troubled region in northern India
4 Those of the highest caste
5 India's principal religion
6 Dry – as in desert conditions
7 India's official language
8 Old system of social segregation
9 Reddish, leached soils
10 City in the west of India
11 Traditional source of power for steel making in Kolkata
12 River on which Kolkata is situated
13 India's type of climate
14 Cash crop to make beverage
15 Tourism is this kind of export
16 Important city in south-east India
17 Species of fish caught off India
18 Great river in northern India
19 The _____ mountains border northern India
20 'Untouchables'
21 Inland city with many modern software industries
22 Indian shanty town
23 Type of farming that gives high yields per hectare
24 Where a famous Golden Temple can be found
25 India's leading fishing region
26 Animal sacred to Hindus
27 Muslim religion
28 Country bordering north-west India
29 Huge city on west coast of India
30 India was once a colony of this Empire
31 Mountains that are called Western or Eastern

Down

A Sea area off India's west coast
B Sea area off India's east coast
C Fertile soil deposited by rivers such as the Ganges
D Huge city in West Bengal

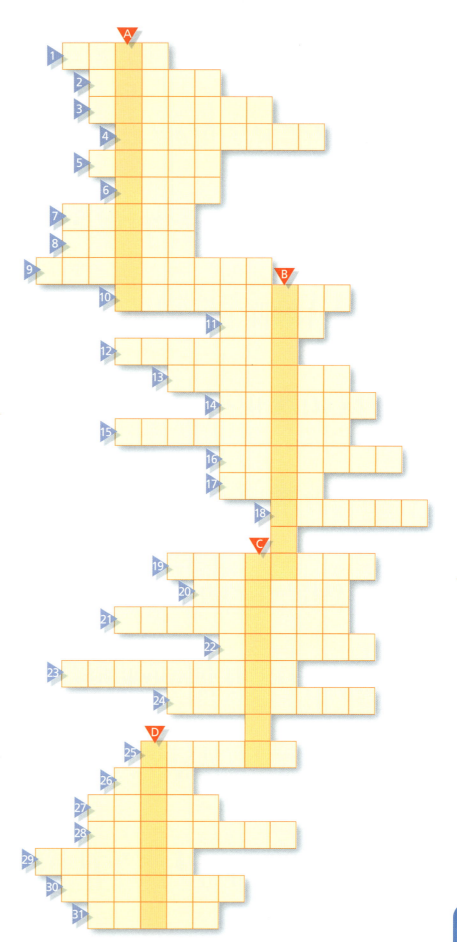

171

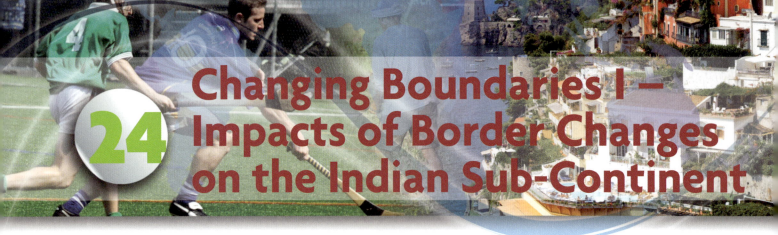

24 Changing Boundaries 1 – Impacts of Border Changes on the Indian Sub-Continent

1   On the outline map provided show and name each of the following:

- India
- Pakistan
- Bangladesh
- the River Indus
- New Delhi
- Dhaka
- Islamabad
- India-controlled Kashmir
- Pakistan-controlled Kashmir.

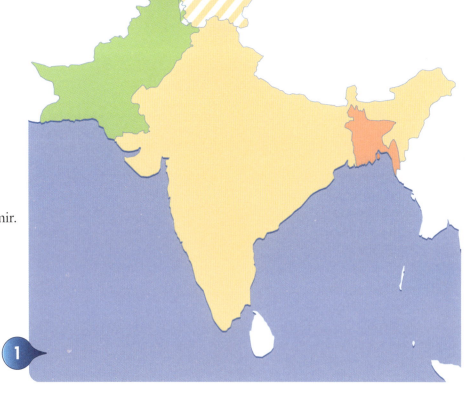

The Indian sub-continent   1

2   Explain how the partition of the British colony of India led to widespread migration in that former colony in 1947.

_____

_____

_____

_____

_____

_____

1 Figure 1 shows areas in Ireland in which at least 25 per cent of people spoke Irish in 1851 and in 2010.

(a) According to Figure 1, in which of the following sets of areas did at least 25 per cent of the people speak Irish (a) in 1850 and (b) in 2010? Indicate your choices by ticking the appropriate boxes.

	1850	2010
(i) Co. Mayo, west Co. Clare, coastal areas of Co. Cork	○	○
(ii) Northwest Co. Mayo, Connemara, Aran Islands	○	○
(iii) Co. Derry, Co. Kerry, Co. Cork	○	○
(iv) Co. Kerry, Connemara, west Co. Donegal	○	○
(v) Co. Dublin, Co. Westmeath, south Co. Wexford	○	○
(vi) Aran Islands, west Dingle peninsula, west Co. Waterford	○	○

(b) Describe some changes that took place between 1851 and 2010 in the borders of Irish- speaking areas* in the province of Munster.

_____

_____

_____

_____

_____

_____

_____

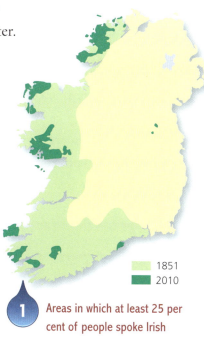

1851
2010

1 Areas in which at least 25 per cent of people spoke Irish

* Areas in which at least 25 per cent of people spoke Irish.

1

Some data relating to EU enlargements					
Expansions	New member countries	Area increase (%)	Population increase (%)	GDP increase (%)	Change in GDP per person (%)
1 Mainly western expansion (1973)	3	31.2	31.9	28.7	-2.9
2 Southern expansions (1981 and 1986)	3	48.3	21.7	15.0	-5.9
3 Mainly northern expansion (1995)	3	42.7	11.1	8.7	1.2
4 Mainly eastern expansions (2004 and 2007)	12	34.4	28.8	8.6	-18.6

1

(a) The table in Figure 1 above refers to four EU expansions numbered 1 to 4.
State which of these expansions resulted in:

(i)   the greatest percentage land increase: _____

(ii) the smallest percentage population increase: _____

(iii) a GDP increase of 15 per cent: _____

(iv) the largest percentage reduction in GDP per person: _____

(b) *'The EU has grown larger and generally poorer over time.'*
Do you think the above statement is true or false?
Explain your answer with reference to Figure 1.

_____

_____

_____

_____

_____

2   Examine the map of European countries in Figure 2.

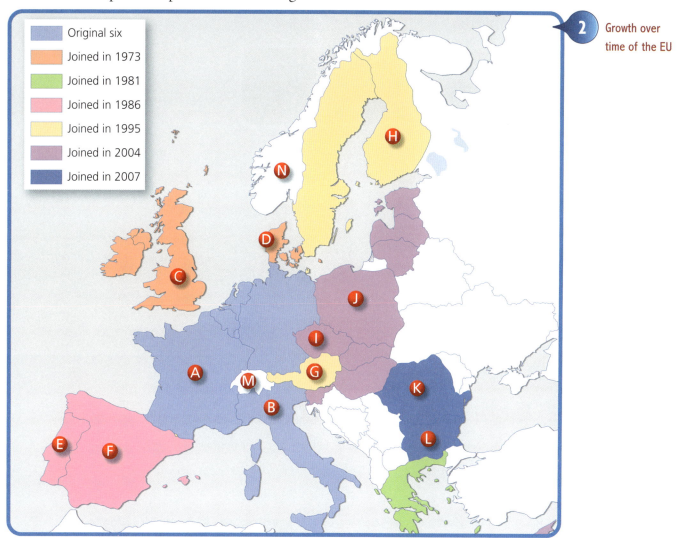

2 Growth over time of the EU

(a)   In the spaces provided, name each of the following:

- The original EU member states labelled **A** and **B**

  A _____   B _____

- The countries **C** and **D** that joined the EU in 1973

  C _____   D _____

- The countries **E** and **F** that joined in 1986

  E _____   F _____

- The countries **G** and **H** that joined in 1995

  G _____   H _____

- The countries **I** and **J** that joined in 2004

  I _____   J _____

- The countries **K** and **L** that joined in 2007

  K _____   L _____

- The countries **M** and **N** that are not members of the EU

  M _____   N _____

(b)   In the spaces provided, write the year in which each of the following countries became a member of the EU:

   Cyprus _____   *Estonia* _____   *Ireland* _____   *Sweden* _____

Exam training
Question with marking scheme and sample answer

3

The question

Discuss the effects of European Union membership on a named EU member state.   (40 marks)

Suggested marking scheme

- Identify (name) EU member state: = 2 marks
- Two effects discussed @ 19 marks each   = 38 marks
  Allocate each set of 19 marks as follows:
  - Identify effect: = 1 mark
  - Discussion: 9 SRPs @ 2 marks each

Total   = 40 marks

> Use this marking scheme to mark the sample answer below. Carefully tick off and mark each 'identification' and SRP that you find. Use the grid that follows the answer to indicate the breakdown of the marks you award.

The <u>Republic of Ireland</u> is a state that was affected in many ways by its membership of the European Union (EU). I will discuss some of the economic and cultural effects of EU membership.

Economic effects

Membership of the EU brought significant economic benefits to Ireland. Some of the greatest economic gains were made by farmers who benefited from the workings of the EU's Common Agricultural Policy (CAP). The CAP's 'intervention' programme bought up surplus agricultural produce at guaranteed prices, thus preventing price collapse in the event of an over-supply of produce. Farmers also received a variety of EU grants and incentives over time. These included 'headage' grants (for units of livestock), special retirement incentives for elderly farmers and 'set-aside' grants for allowing surplus marginal land to go unused. Farmers also benefited from the fact that the EU provided a large tariff-free market for Irish agricultural products.

When Ireland joined the EU in 1973, it was one of the Union's poorest countries. It therefore benefited greatly from EU financial assistance. Such assistance was financed by the European Regional Development Fund. Much of it came from Structural Funds and Cohesion Funds, which were set up to improve infrastructure such as roads and to create much-needed employment. Throughout the early 1990s up to 80 per cent of Ireland's major road upgrades were paid for by EU grants. Such aid diminished, however, when Ireland's economy boomed between the late 1990s and 2008 and when the EU expanded to include many poorer Southern and Eastern European countries.

Cultural effects

EU membership has helped to make Ireland much more multicultural in its population make-up and outlook. Prior to its entry into Europe in 1973, Ireland was a rather monocultural country that clung proudly to its nationalistic and Gaelic traditions. These traditions now tend to be more mixed with the cultural traditions of other Europeans with whom our people have mingled as EU citizens.

The expansion of the EU towards Eastern Europe in 2004 and 2007 had particularly big cultural effects on Ireland. These expansions brought ten former Communist countries, including Poland, Latvia and Lithuania, into the EU and helped to open the door for workers from these countries to migrate to Ireland. Between 2002 and 2006, the number of Polish people living in Ireland increased from fewer than 20,000 to more than 60,000. These and migrants from other EU countries have had several cultural effects on our country.

- A variety of European languages are now more commonly used in Ireland. For example, mass is now celebrated in Polish in several Irish Catholic churches, where Polish people celebrate feasts such as Easter with ceremonies that are unique to Polish traditions. Our Leaving Certificate examinations now offer a much wider variety of languages, including Polish, Latvian, Lithuanian and Czech.

- Many Polish and other non-Irish-national 'ethnic' shops now operate in cities and towns throughout the country. These shops sell foods and other 'home country' products to immigrants in Ireland, thereby enriching the cultural diversity of our land.

- Many EU immigrants have now settled permanently in Ireland and some have married Irish people. They are likely to leave more permanent cultural imprints in the country. Their children tend to be bilingual (or trilingual if they can speak Irish) and many of them tend to blend some cultural traits of their immigrant parent(s) with aspects of Gaelic culture such as playing hurling and Gaelic football.

Marks awarded		
Identification of **member state**		
Effect One:		
	Effect stated	
	Discussion	
Effect Two:		
	Effect stated	
	Discussion	
Total marks awarded		

4 Name and explain **two** impacts on Ireland of the enlargement
of the European Union. (30 marks)

*Frequently
asked question*

_____

_____

_____

_____

_____

_____

_____

_____

_____

_____

_____

_____

_____

_____

_____

_____

_____

_____

Official Leaving Certificate marking scheme

- Impacts identified: 2 + 2 marks   = 4 marks
- Examination: 13 SRPs @ 2 marks each
  (up to 7 SRPs for one impact and up to
  6 SRPs for the other)   = 26 marks

                                                 = **30 marks**

Total

Hints

- Examination without reference to Ireland
  would score no mark.
- Examination without reference to EU
  enlargement would score a maximum of
  6 SRPs.
- Try to exceed the number of SRPs required.

27 Political, Economic and Cultural Interactions in a Divided Ireland

1 In the spaces provided, mach each item in **Column X** with the appropriate item in **Column Y**.

Column X	
1	The Government of Ireland Act
2	Gerrymandering
3	UDA
4	Belfast Agreement
5	EEC
6	Harland and Wolff

Column Y	
A	North–South Ministerial Council
B	Discrimination
C	Partition
D	Common Market
E	Shipbuilding in Belfast
F	Loyalist paramilitary group

1	
2	
3	
4	
5	
6	

2 Each of the items or events listed below has influenced human interactions in Ireland. For each item, indicate whether you think *political*, *economic* or *cultural* interactions were the most strongly influenced. Indicate your choices by ticking the appropriate boxes.

	Political	Economic	Cultural
● Belfast (Good Friday) Agreement	◯	◯	◯
● Derry City Airport	◯	◯	◯
● Dublin–Belfast motorway	◯	◯	◯
● European Union	◯	◯	◯
● GAA	◯	◯	◯
● Gerrymandering	◯	◯	◯
● Government of Ireland Act	◯	◯	◯
● Irish Rugby Football Union (IRFU)	◯	◯	◯
● North–South Ministerial Council	◯	◯	◯
● 'Protectionist' policies	◯	◯	◯

3 (a) The pie charts in Figure 1 show the number of manufacturing jobs in Northern Ireland and in the Republic of Ireland in 1960, 1989 and 2007. Use the information given to fill in the gaps and to circle the correct *alternatives* in the passage given below.

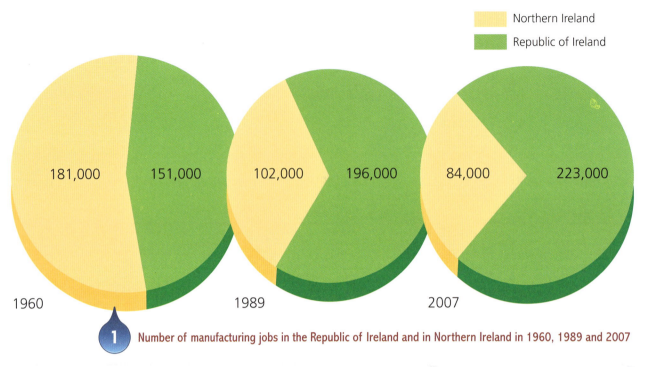

▢ Northern Ireland
▢ Republic of Ireland

181,000   151,000   102,000   196,000   84,000   223,000

1960   1989   2007

1   Number of manufacturing jobs in the Republic of Ireland and in Northern Ireland in 1960, 1989 and 2007

The pie charts indicate a steady *increase / decrease* in manufacturing jobs in Northern Ireland from _____ jobs in 1960 to _____ jobs in 1989 to _____ jobs in 2007. This represents a total *increase / decrease* of more than *100 / 200* per cent within a *47 / 37*-year period.

By contrast, the pie charts show a *steady / overall* increase over time in the number of manufacturing jobs in the Republic of Ireland. In the 29 years from 1960, manufacturing jobs there increased from _____ jobs to _____ jobs, giving a total increase of _____ jobs. Between 1989 and 2007, the number of manufacturing jobs in the Republic *increased / decreased* to _____.

The total number of manufacturing jobs in the island of Ireland *increased / decreased* from *332,000 / 185,000* jobs in 1960 to _____ thousand jobs in 1989. This represented an *increase / decrease* of _____ thousand jobs and mirrors a period of severe industrial decline in *Northern Ireland / the Republic of Ireland*.

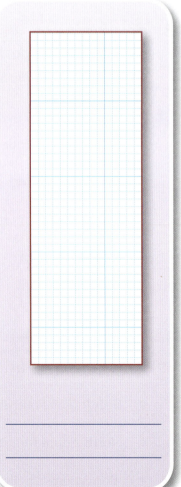

(b) Use the squared paper to create a bar chart that illustrates the number of manufacturing jobs in the Republic of Ireland in 1960 (as given in Figure 1). Your bar chart must include a labelled vertical axis and a title.

Advice Section

The pages that follow offer some tips and explanations that may be useful in preparing for your Leaving Certificate Geography exam.

Preparing for your exam

Be prepared

Only careful preparation will enable you to reach your full potential in the Leaving Certificate Geography examination. Careful preparation means **steady work and study** that should begin at the start of fifth year and continue up to the Leaving Certificate exam. Remember that **any** part of the course – including everything you learn throughout fifth year – could potentially appear on the Geography examination paper.

The two most important elements of steady work are:

1   Taking an active part in each **lesson.** That means listening, asking questions and contributing to the lesson.

2   Following a clear timetable of evening **study.** Make sure that this timetable includes a daily period for studying Geography.

> **In class:**
> 1   **Listen** to the contributions of your fellow students as well as to your teacher.
> 2   **Contribute** in class when appropriate.
> 3   Ask **questions** on any points that you do not understand.

	Monday	Tueday	Wednesday	Thursday	Friday	Saturday
5.00–5.40pm						9.30–10.30am
5.40–6.10	Geog					10.40–11.40am
6.10–6.40				Geog		
7.30–8.10						
8.10–8.40			Geog			
9.00–9.30		Geog			Geog	
9.30–9.50						

For essays and /or occasional extra revision

One student's study timetable showing periods for Geography study.

This timetable has been tailored to the needs of an individual student, so it not recommended that you try to copy it exactly. But note these positive aspects:

●   Study is interspersed with an evening meal and a planned short break. These breaks help to prevent fatigue and so assist concentration.

●   Geography is allocated different times on different evenings. It is not always given 'preferential' treatment at the beginning of study or 'downtime' at the end of study.

More about homework/study

- Regular and diligent homework is a **vital** element of effective learning. It is often the element that is least well carried out.
- Homework is *not solely written homework*. **Learning and revising** what has been covered in class are important aspects of effective homework.
- Learning and revision demands **real and concentrated effort.** It is not sufficient to 'read over' material that needs to be learned.
- Follow a **steady and regular homework timetable** (see example on page 182). Avoid sporadic periods of 'panic' learning. Remember that the *quality* of study time is as important as the length of time spent studying.

Homework working conditions

- If possible, do your homework in a **quiet** room.
- Telephone calls should **not** be made or taken during homework time. This is important!
- A television should **not** be on while you are doing homework.
- It is best to do your homework in silence. Background music is **not** recommended.

On the day of your Geography examination

1 **Be on time.** Take your place in the examination hall some minutes before the exam is due to begin. Write your examination number on your answer books before the exam begins. Wait calmly for the paper to be distributed. Focus your mind quietly on the task at hand.

2 **Be equipped.** Bring the following to the examination:
- At least *two blue or black ink pens.* (Some ballpoint pens may not be suitable for extensive writing. To write with them you must force in the tiny ball at the tip of the pen and this, over time, can cause soreness of the wrist or hand.)
- Two pre-sharpened 'medium to soft' *pencils* (for drawing diagrams).
- A pencil eraser.
- A 30cm transparent plastic *ruler*.
- A reliable *watch*. Each examination centre should have a functioning clock, but it is safer not to depend on it. You may need your watch for the essential task of timing your examination questions.
- A (yellow) highlighter.
- One *red biro* (optional).

Things you do <u>NOT</u> need in exams

X *Lots of coloured pens and pencils*
Geographical diagrams should be relevant, clear and well labelled. But they do *not* need to be coloured. The 'comfort colouring' of diagrams gains no extra marks and is therefore a waste of valuable time.

X *Correction fluid*
The use of correction fluid can be another waste of exam time. If you need to erase something you have written, simply cross it out.

---

3 **Be focused.** After two years of study and preparation you should be well prepared for your exam. Try to remain *coolly focused* on the task at hand.

The structure of the Higher Level examination paper

PART ONE

Short-answer questions   **80 marks**

You must answer at least ten out of **12 short-answer questions.**   **80 marks**

- Each short-answer question carries *8 marks.*
- It is best to *attempt all 12* questions – you will be marked on your ten best answers.
- These questions are all based on the *core sections* of the course – Physical Geography, Regional Geography and Geographical Skills.

PART TWO

Section 1 – Core
Physical Geography

Three structured (multi-part*) questions to **answer one only**   **80 marks**

Regional Geography

Three structured (multi-part*) questions to **answer one only**   **80 marks**

Section 2 – Electives

You will have studied the *Economic Activities* **or** the *Human Environment* elective.

Each elective will feature:

Three structured (multi-part*) questions to **answer one only**   **80 marks**

Section 3 – Options

You will have studied **one** of the following options:

Global Interdependence **or** *Geoecology* **or** *Culture and Identity* **or** *The Atmosphere–Ocean Environment.*

Each option will feature **three** essay-type questions to **answer one only**   **80 marks**

                                                      Total: 400 marks

---

* What is a 'structured' or multi-part question?

Each of these questions consists of three parts:

- Part A – a mainly skill-based question   20 marks
- Part B – usually a knowledge-based question   30 marks
- Part C – usually a knowledge-based question   30 marks

Total: **80 marks**

The structure of the Ordinary Level examination paper

PART ONE

Short-answer questions

You must answer at least ten of **12 short-answer questions.**   **100 marks**

- Each short-answer question carries *10 marks.*
- It is best to *attempt all 12* questions – you will be marked on your ten best answers.
- These questions are all based on the *core sections* of the course – Physical Geography, Regional Geography and Geographical Skills

PART TWO

Section 1 – Core
Physical Geography

Three structured (multi-part*) questions to **answer one only**   **100 marks**

Physical Geography

Three structured (multi-part*) questions to **answer one only**   **100 marks**

Section 2 – Electives

You will have studied the *Economic Activities* **or** the *Human Environment* elective.

Each elective will feature:

Three structured (multi-part*) questions to **answer one only**   **100 marks**

Total: 400 marks

> *** What is a 'structured' or multi-part question?**
>
> Each of these questions consists of three parts:
> - Part A – a mainly skill-based question   30 marks
> - Part B – usually a knowledge-based question   30/40 marks
> - Part C – usually a knowledge-based question   30/40 marks
>
> **Total:**   **100 marks**

Timing – a vital examination skill

It is essential that you complete all parts of all questions required of you in the Leaving Certificate examination. To ensure this, you must follow a plan that determines the amount of time to be allocated to each question and part of a question that you answer.

Suggested timing schemes are given here for Higher and for Ordinary Level Leaving Certificate Geography. You do not *have* to follow either of these particular schemes. You or your teacher might devise an alternative scheme that suits you better. What *is* important is that you practise and stick to a suitable plan of examination timing.

Suggested timing scheme – Higher Level

Total time available for the examination is 2 hours and 50 minutes (170 minutes).

Timing allocations

- Reading and selecting questions (see box)   *10 minutes*

- Question One (**short-answer questions**)   *20 minutes*

- Question Two (**Core – Physical Geography multi-part* question**)   *35 minutes*

- Question Three (**Core – Economic Geography multi-part* question**)   *35 minutes*

- Question Four (**Elective – multi-part* question**)   *35 minutes*

- Question Five (**Option – essay-type question**)   *35 minutes*

    Total time   *170 minutes*

> *** Time allocation for each multi-part question:**
> - 20-mark section   9 minutes
> - First 30-mark section   13 minutes
> - Second 30-mark section   13 minutes

> **Reading and selecting questions**
> - It is very important that you begin the examination by **reading** the exam paper carefully. Pay particular attention to the questions that appear in *Part Two* of the paper. In the case of the Elective and Option sections, concentrate *only* on the Elective and Option that you have studied.
> - Having read the relevant selections, **choose** the questions that you will answer in Part Two of the paper. **Read** these selected questions **again** and carefully highlight the key words in each question.
> - Take **up to ten minutes** to *read*, *select* and *highlight*.

Suggested timing scheme – Ordinary Level

Total time available for the examination is 2 hours and 50 minutes (170 minutes).

Timing allocations

- Reading and selecting questions (see box) *10 minutes*

- Question One (**short-answer questions**) *25 minutes*

- Question Two (**Core – Physical Geography multi-part* question**) *45 minutes*

- Question Three (**Core – Economic Geography multi-part* question**) *45 minutes*

- Question Four (**Elective – multi-part* question**) *45 minutes*

  Total time *170 minutes*

* Time allocation for each multi-part question:
- First 30-mark section 13 minutes
- Second 30-mark section 13 minutes
- 40-mark section 19 minutes

Reading and selecting questions

- It is very important that you begin the examination by **reading** the exam paper carefully. Pay particular attention to the questions that appear in *Part Two* of the paper. In the case of the Elective section, concentrate only on the Elective that you have studied.

- Having read the relevant selections, **choose** the questions that you will answer in Part Two of the paper. **Read** again these selected questions **again** and carefully **highlight** the key words in each question.

- Take **up to ten minutes** to *read*, *select* and *highlight*.

i 226 63538

Some advice on . . .

Questions students often ask about the Leaving Certificate Geography exam

- *In which order should I answer the exam questions?*

You should, with your teacher's help, decide this for yourself. As a general rule, however, it is best to begin with the question you consider to be the easiest and most quickly done. Many students judge these to be the short-answer questions in Part One of the exam. Always leave the most difficult or potentially 'longest' question until last.

- *What should I do if a question is taking longer than its allocated time? Should I persevere and finish it or should I move on to another question?*

Unless you can finish a question *very* quickly after its allocated time it is better to move on. It is very important that you do not run out of time at the end of the exam and therefore fail to attempt all the required questions.

- *What should I do if I finish the exam early?*

Read through the answers you have written and try to add some extra relevant material to them. This extra material sometimes lifts candidates' results to a higher grade. Remember that while you are still in the exam room you could be inspired with some extra ideas or remember some extra relevant facts. When you leave you give up any chance of improving your answers. So *never* leave an exam early.

- *What if the exam is unusually difficult?*

If this happens the most important thing is to keep cool and answer the required questions as well and as fully as possible. Remember that it will be equally difficult for all candidates to do well in an unusually difficult examination. This *may* cause the exam to he marked rather more leniently than usual. A cool and focused student who perseveres in tackling a difficult exam can therefore turn difficulty into opportunity.